FOOD FOR THE SOUL

Brian D'Arcy CP

Food for the Soul

Best wishes always

Brian D'arcy CP

the columba press

First published in 2013 by

the columba press

55A Spruce Avenue,
Stillorgan Industrial Park,
Blackrock, Co. Dublin

Cover by sin é design
Cover image by Lunny Imaging
Origination by The Columba Press
Printed by Bell & Bain Ltd

ISBN 978 1 78218 086 9

CONTENTS

INTRODUCTION

Plato believed that knowledge is food for the soul while Jesus said human beings do not live on bread alone. I don't disagree with either of them but from my own lived experience I can testify that anguish, rejection and the pain of abandonment will destroy your soul. I think I may have survived this dark night by the skin of my teeth.

Food for the Soul, in a series of random chapters, charts the spiritual path which helped me through the most devastating faith-crisis of my life.

In 2010 I was formally censured by the Congregation for the Doctrine of the Faith (CDF). The then head of that congregation wrote to the Superior General of The Passionists (the religious order of which I am a member) that my writings and broadcasts had been 'a source of great scandal to the faithful'. As a result I received a formal canonical warning to cease being critical of the Vatican. I was ordered not to question the Magisterium or the disciplines of the Catholic Church.

At this point let me emphasise that I've always been at pains not to contradict the formal teachings of the Catholic Church, in my writings and broadcasts in the secular media. For that reason, I requested to the publisher that the text of this book be given to a theologian for comment prior to publication.

As a matter of record I need to clarify that the CDF never communicated with me directly and never indicated who was 'scandalised' by what I wrote. I was warned that I could be excommunicated if I didn't abide by the CDF's rules.

For three years now this censure has eaten me up inside and destroyed me as a human being and as a priest. The foundations of my faith were shattered. An institution which treats people in such a threatening way does not, it seems to me, act in accordance with gospel principles. This is not the Catholic Church I gave my life to. It is not the church I love and serve.

I was indeed critical of the way church leadership handled the child sex abuse scandals in Ireland and elsewhere – and I was absolutely correct to do so. I am a survivor of clerical sex abuse myself. I have been through enough personal devastation to recognise that secrecy is lethal when dealing with abusers.

Like all concerned Catholics I was critical of the Vatican's approach to church governance on the grounds that it lacked compassion and was not as Christ intended it. I am convinced I was correct to highlight these obvious shortcomings also.

Indeed Pope Francis has rightly confirmed that what went on was truly scandalous and has repeatedly offered more stringent criticism of the evils of clericalism than I have done. He promises to bring about the necessary changes too.

For three years I have struggled, not always successfully, with what happened to me and other loyal priests in Ireland; I've thought seriously about leaving the active ministry. I was forced to embark upon a long process of discernment. It was a painful, lonely journey but I am convinced there is no other way to handle genuine doubt in a positive way.

Had it not been for the thousands of letters I received pleading with me not to give up, I could now be 'a former priest'. I was greatly helped too by an in-depth documentary BBC Television undertook with me (*The Turbulent Priest*) which pushed me to my limits and allowed me to share the truth of what happened with a mass audience.

To survive I had to find a sustaining faith, a spiritual life, which was meaningful, real and based on the theology of the Passion – a way of living and being, which had truth and integrity at its centre. Faith, I learned, is not something we lose; rather there comes a time when we just stop shaping our lives by it.

With professional help I concluded that I am called to write, broadcast and preach without such interference. Meaningful communication is founded on the ability to speak the truth. As an essential part of being true to gospel values, I searched for a spirituality which was based on genuine human freedom; I am still searching.

Slowly, I have begun to live and act confidently again. I recognise that nobody can *give* me back my freedom; I have to *choose* freedom for myself. Slow, painful, baby steps along the dark, twisted road to enlightenment, become nourishing food for my soul.

That's where this book comes from. It's not a controversial book. And it's not about how the Vatican dealt with me (and is still dealing with me). Rather it's an attempt to share an accessible spirituality with anyone struggling to overcome disillusionment. I believe there are many disillusioned people in the Catholic Church who long for encouragement, not condemnation, and I hope they'll find a kindred soul in these pages. We need a God we can trust; we need spirituality which heals.

Much of the material in this book is gleaned from broadcasts and writings. But mostly it comes from my reflections on the Sunday readings which I share every week with our supportive, prayerful community of believers at St Gabriel's Retreat, The Graan in Enniskillen.

Hope, like bereavement, does not follow a straight path. Times of enlightenment are followed quickly by periods of darkness. Both are natural processes which take their own course. The chapters therefore, do not follow a chronological path. Dates at the beginning of certain chapters let the reader know the context in which I was writing at the time. There is some repetition because each chapter is complete in itself. Phrases like 'present church leadership' could refer to the reign of Benedict or Francis, depending on the date.

These years of discernment have, I know, made me a humbler, more rooted human being. I'm a better, more compassionate priest too. I'm far from perfect – thank God. But then I don't have to be perfect; God loves me as I am in my imperfection and vulnerability. I need God. When no one else can be trusted, it's good to have discovered a God who is Trust.

I know I wouldn't have survived these dark days without the prayers and support of decent Christian people from all over the world. The quiet support of a few genuine priest friends was particularly helpful as was the tangible support of my family and friends.

I learned to hang on to crumbs of wisdom which fell from many tables. For example, Fr Jim Cogley sent me some chapters from a book he was writing, to read over and comment upon. In one chapter he wrote about four common responses to a faith crisis.

a)   We can *ignore* the problem by burying our heads in the sand.
b)   *Deplore* the situation we're in by blaming others (even justifiably). This is 'fixing the blame rather than fixing the problem'.
c)   *Restore*. That is to attempt to return to the way things were in the past without questioning whether they ever worked or whether they will work in our new world order.
d)   *Explore*. Face the present crisis, ask the relevant questions, and see the possibilities for a future based on hope. (*Wood You Believe*, Volume Six by Fr Jim Cogley)

I lived all the above!

Then the miracle happened ... When I was at my lowest ebb physically and spiritually at the start of 2013, something truly extraordinary happened. Benedict XVI graciously resigned from the papacy.

When the cardinals met in conclave the Holy Spirit surprised us again and guided them to act fearlessly. Amazingly they quickly elected a cardinal from South America, Jorge Bergoglio, who, for the first time in history, took the name Francis. From his first appearance on the balcony of St Peter's Square, it was obvious this Pope was different in the same way that Pope John XXIII was different. Both were God's gift to a broken church.

On the evening Francis was elected I was filled with the kind of hope which can only come from God. Almost instantly the darkness lifted as Pope Francis displayed a compassion which was life-giving to believers and doubters alike.

As the days and weeks have passed, he has become a spiritual leader who lives in, knows and blesses our world. He lives simply, speaks honestly, acts compassionately and leads bravely.

Now it is the Pope himself who is highlighting the short-comings of church structures and it is the Pope who is proposing changes remarkably similar to those for which I, and others, am being censured.

Pope Francis has reshaped priorities bringing compassion and personal warmth to the fore. Like the father of the prodigal son, he celebrates forgiveness in a most meaningful way.

There will be difficult days but I've always believed that until we accept what we are, we cannot plan to become what we should be.

Food for the Soul is an attempt to express my quest for a practical spirituality which would take me through the crisis I was plunged into. Somewhere along that painful journey I made a decision not to waste the rest of my life in anger and resentment. I now know I can manage this journey of faith in a positive way.

In his now famous interview for Jesuit publications (September 2013), Pope Francis urged everyone of goodwill not to abandon the church despite its obvious failings, but rather to, 'Think with the church'. We should not allow ourselves to believe that, 'thinking with the church means only thinking with the hierarchy of the church ... the church is the totality of God's people,' he said. True holiness is in the patience of the people of God ... 'this was the sanctity of my parents, my mum and my dad, my grandmother Rose who loved me so much'.

I can identify with this homely insight from Pope Francis. I received the gift of faith from my parents and I model my priesthood on their legacy to me. Following the Pope's advice I want to experience the mercy and compassion of God so that I can help others in their time of need.

Like him I believe, 'the church we should be thinking about is the home of all, not just a small chapel which can hold only a small group of selected people … [what] the church needs most today is the ability to heal wounds, to warm the hearts of the faithful.'

Powerfully, he spelt out what the church needs: 'The people of God want pastors, not clergy acting like bureaucrats or government officials.' To prove his point he asks us to consider a practical question. 'When God looks at a gay person does he endorse the person with love or reject and condemn the person? … it is necessary to accompany them with mercy. When that happens the Holy Spirit inspires the priest to say the right thing.'

That's the language I've longed to hear from Rome. It's a language I understand, it's a truly pastoral approach showing us the compassion of a loving God which all of us, especially priests, must be free to preach and to put into practice in our ministry.

I hope you will recognise yourself in these pages and that you too will find food for your soul.

Brian D'Arcy
29 September 2013,
The Fiftieth Anniversary of my First Profession

ALL CHANGE?

4 August 2013

It is a constant call of the gospel to re-examine our lives, our values, our sense of worth and to reflect on where the choices we make lead us.

The gospel frequently reminds us that we don't have a permanent home on this earth. To live as if we do is the ultimate 'foolish' attitude. We know our lives can change in a flash.

I was thinking during the week that less than a year ago the Catholic Church was a hostile place for many of us to live in. The disillusionment had been coming slowly; the stark reality of where we were was clawing at the heart of our belief. The institutional church, particularly as represented by Rome, seemed to stifle all dialogue, all hope, all initiative. It's no exaggeration for me personally to say that I felt a complete stranger in the official church to which I had given my life. The language of the new missal, the rigidity of thought and commentary, the stifling of dialogue, the absence of justice – all of these suggested to us that the official church was more interested in canon law than in representing the values of Jesus Christ. Many Catholics throughout the world, for the first time in their lives, felt abandoned.

Then, against all the odds, Pope Benedict too must have realised that what was happening in and around the official structures of the church was corrupt and deceptive, even to him. In a wonderful moment of spiritual bravery he resigned from being Pope. It was a huge decision and was undoubtedly the work of the Holy Spirit.

None of us though expected his successor to be much different. So many of the bishops and cardinals were of the same mentality that it seemed impossible to have a change of direction.

Then Pope Francis came along. Few of us expected him to be elected, none of us dreamt that he would take the name Francis and none of us thought that he could change so much simply by being human, humble and, in a sense, ordinary. It was his smile, his humility in asking for prayers, his ability to get rid of all the trappings and live a normal life. His way of expressing compassion and love and making the poor a priority didn't change any of the laws, but certainly did change the direction of the church.

This past week was a real eye-opener (Pope Francis' trip to South America). Perhaps he was encouraged by the three million young people he met in Brazil, perhaps it was enthusiasm regained by going back to South America, the South America that he knew and loved. Whatever the reason his press conference on the plane back to Rome was a complete revelation. His language to the young people in Rio, as well as on the plane, was that Catholics should be proud to be Catholics, that they should continue 'to shake up the status quo'. That we should live on the margins of life. We should speak about our faith in an ordinary way and not over-intellectualise it. We should spread the message of love, compassion and forgiveness.

He admitted the church has appeared to be weak and far too distant from the ordinary people we're supposed to communicate with. The church is too concerned about its own existence as an institution rather than being the mouthpiece and a home for those seeking the Kingdom of God. He admitted too that the church in its present constitution was not capable of facing the questions of life all around us. He was harsh on priests and bishops who are mere careerists. He told us that we should be among the people, working with them and listening to them.

And then he used the word *gay*. He didn't change any of the rules but at least he admitted that when God made somebody with a certain orientation 'who was he to judge them'? We were disappointed when he said he felt that after John Paul II it will be impossible to have women priests. But then he said we needed a theology of women and for women in the church. That was an inspired insight because, hopefully, theology will lead us to a different view of priesthood too. It was an admission that we need a fresh theology which had been practically abandoned for the past thirty years. Theologians who pushed the boundaries were silenced; canon lawyers were promoted. Now Pope Francis is saying that we need to develop theology itself.

All of this shows us that in the twinkling of an eye things can change and those of us who felt outside the church, now feel the Pope himself is saying the same thing as we are. In fact I thought that I should write to Pope Francis soon and warn him that if he keeps saying the things he's now saying he'll be censured too.

HANS KÜNG ON POPE FRANCIS

9 June 2013

One of the most influential theologians of the modern era is Fr Hans Küng. He's had his battles with the Vatican, especially Pope John Paul II. In his early career he was a colleague and good friend of Joseph Ratzinger, who later, as Cardinal Ratzinger, was responsible for removing Hans Küng from teaching in Catholic Universities. When Ratzinger became Pope Benedict, the two men tried to reconcile their differences but without much success.

Hans Küng is still a priest and theologian in good standing and as an eighty-five-year-old academic has been reflecting on the changes Pope Francis is attempting to bring about in the Vatican's structure.

Firstly, the name Francis is significant. St Francis of Assisi is one of the most iconic saints in the Catholic Church. In the thirteenth century he was a fun-loving and worldly child of a rich textile merchant in Assisi. But at the age of twenty-four he gave up his family's wealth to preach the gospel of Jesus Christ to the poor.

According to Küng, Pope Francis is attempting to live simply in the midst of wealth, in the same way as his patron saint did. Like Francis he will need to speak the language of the people and emphasise his own humanity. Küng concludes, he will be 'a Pope who demonstrates he is a man with his feet on the ground'.

Küng quoting church history, notes that during the life of Francis of Assisi, his contemporary, Pope Innocent III, would not approve the rule of the founder of the Franciscans. Innocent III 'was a man of worldly power, a born ruler, a distinguished theologian, a shrewd lawyer, a clever speaker and a capable administrator,' according to Küng. He gave a new status to the Papacy – that of 'absolute ruler, law-giver and judge of Christianity'. Küng sums up the situation brilliantly: 'Already in his time there were signs of decay which up until our own time, have remained features of the Roman Curia system: Nepotism, favouritism, acquisitiveness, corruption and dubious financial dealings.'

Francis of Assisi wanted to challenge positions of privilege, great wealth, and worldly power. He wanted the gospel to be taken seriously by all – lay and clerical alike. According to Küng, the Franciscan ideal, if it is to be taken seriously, must be 'about poverty, humility and simplicity'.

To follow the ideals of St Francis, the Pope will have to leave aside pomp and circumstance and, in the spirit of Francis, have a transparent church whose leaders live frugally. The church should concern itself above all with the poor, the weak and the marginalised.

A church rooted in worldly powers is a church which highlights dogma, moralistic censor and legal hedging. The church of Francis means 'a church of good news, of joy, a theology based radically on gospel values, a church that listens to people instead of indoctrinating them from above, a church that does not only teach but one that constantly learns'.

St Francis died on 3 October 1226 at the age of forty-four. He died as poor as he had lived. In contrast Innocent III, for all his power and status, died unexpectedly at the age of fifty-six in 1216. He had been rejected by those within the system he himself established. 'This Pope who had known how to increase the power, property and wealth of the Holy See, like no other before him, was found dead deserted by all, naked and robbed by his own servants,' Küng recalls.

The task ahead for Pope Francis is to re-organise the Roman Curia which has brought such degradation to our beloved church.

Reform of the structures of the church will be widely supported. To do so though, will mean reforms coming from the bottom up; they will have to be implemented with or without the approval of the hierarchy or the Curia.

This generation has been given a time of grace to reform and to turn back to Christ. The careerists have had their day. The Holy Spirit will now regenerate a church to be proud of.

The Cherry Blossoms

22 April 2012

This morning I went for a walk just to enjoy the beauty of this time of year. When I came back in I got a jolt. I looked at the front page of the *Independent* and saw the headline, 'Church wants D'Arcy to apologise for the F word.' Strangely enough I didn't know they knew my opinion on feminism which seems to be the F word which disturbs them most. However I was relieved to read a little further down that it was Ray D'Arcy and not Brian D'Arcy they were talking about.

That distracted me from what was on my mind. Outside there were beautiful blossoms, particularly on the cherry trees. And it got me thinking again about an incident which has been coming back to me in recent weeks.

Fifty years ago this year when I first entered The Graan as a seventeen-year-old boy, I tried to be a good novice. I accepted that the old (though very young) Brian D'Arcy had to die and that I had to accept a new name which was Desmond Mary. I left my clothes to be locked up by the Novice Master and put on used, penitential clothes, a habit and sandals.

I accepted that the food was awful and that there was very little of it. I accepted that I had to get up in the middle of the night to pray and then go back to bed before getting up at six again. I accepted many of those things. As well as silence, I had to leave my family behind. I could not write to them and I could not speak to them if they came to church. I should not try to understand what was happening in the world. It was tough but I accepted it all. I knew it was what I had to do to be a priest. Now I realise it was seriously damaging to me as a human being.

One day when I was a novice the rector called me to his cell (room). The rector had been in Africa and was very close to being made a bishop. He was educated in Rome and was secretary to the Passionist general for years. He came home, served as provincial and now was rector at The Graan. He was a man of some standing.

The Novices Master was away so the rector was in charge of us. In his room he asked me if I could use a cross-cut saw. I could, because my father had taught me. He then asked another novice, if he could use the saw. He said he could even though he couldn't, because he was afraid to tell the truth.

The rector then gave us a task. Outside the monastery there was a row of twenty beautiful cherry trees. They had been planted ten to fifteen years earlier. They were a good size and they were beautiful in blossom. He then ordered me to cut all twenty of them down as close to the ground as possible. They were, in his words, 'useless trees that gathered dirt'.

We went to the farmyard, got a cross-cut and I explained to my companion how it worked. We started to cut the trees and by midday we had all twenty trees knocked down. The rest of the novices came out after lunch and carried them to the dump where they were left to dry out before they were burned. We were happy with our work.

Some of the community berated us for daring to cut the trees, even though they knew we had to obey the rector. They were afraid to talk to the rector so they rounded on us instead.

All went well until the next day when I was at solitary walk – a time when we walked around for thirty minutes and every now and then stopped to recall the presence of God. It was a reminder that you shouldn't look at nature but instead try to contemplate God. Another example of dualistic spirituality.

Whilst I was walking, Charlie Keenan, who was the gardener, walked over to me. I didn't know that Charlie was the man who originally planted those trees, carefully nurtured them and was very proud to see them blossoming. It was the work of a lifetime. He looked at me with anger in his eyes. As he stuck a grape in the ground he said, 'Are you the lunatic who cut down the cherry trees?' Since I was not allowed to speak I nodded in assent. 'Well it's jail you should get. Only a lunatic or a criminal would cut down such beautiful trees.' And he went back to his work. The presence of God was far from my mind.

Only then did I realise the mistake I'd made!

But I was seventeen, innocent, eager to please and under obedience. If I hadn't cut the trees I could have been sent home. Today I think it's probably the most serious sin I have committed in my life. How could I not understand that it is a sin to destroy God's beauty?

The poet Thomas Bracken has a line which says, 'Poor souls with stunted vision, oft measure giants by their own narrow gauge.' The rector, who spent years in Rome, in the midst of the greatest art treasures of the world, and who had travelled the world, had decided that a beautiful creation like a cherry tree was dirt. Charlie Keenan, a man of nature, a man of the soil, a man in touch with God's power, knew that they were a work of art and should not be destroyed.

I can't claim that I understood exactly the implications of it all at the time. But as I think of it now I recognise that God was teaching me about the limits to human obedience. I did the right thing but an evil thing. As the gospel says, 'God's love comes to perfection ... peace be with you.'

So how do we cope with the difficulties, tragedies, perhaps the disasters of one's life? Like the disciples the first way of coping seems to be fear. It's as old as mankind. Evil comes to us and fear is the result. We are crippled by fear and despair. In the Book of Genesis we are told that when Adam and Eve committed sin, 'They hid themselves because they were afraid.' Ever since God is endeavouring throughout history to rid us of that despair by offering us forgiveness and hope. The antidote to fear is to have trust and to accept peace. The Resurrection greeting is, 'Peace be with you.'

In the gospels we see how Jesus preached to people. It was not in a legalistic way. Jesus helped people in a human way. He walked with them. He made the journey with those in despair. He listened to them. He let them touch his woundedness. He made himself vulnerable in their presence and then he ate a meal with them and shared stories and explained life around the table.

We all have the experience of dealing with life's disappointments. We understand what crushed hope is. Will I have a job? Will he/she get better? How will I mend a broken relationship? As we look through the gospels we learn how Jesus helps us.

1. Our journeys and doubts are good. God walks with us and because he does, our journey is a journey of discovery.
2. Jesus doesn't jump in to take away our pain. He allows us to recognise that pain is part of our redemption.
3. When we have a crisis, if accepted in the right spirit, it will be a holy experience. A crossroads where we can make new choices and discover a new life.
4. Each of us lives a series of stories. We have little stories that form big pictures. Upon reflection the little stories have a pattern and show us how we can learn from each of them. We live our lives looking to the future but we only understand our lives with the benefit of hindsight. A long time afterwards we understand what we have been through.

Today is an invitation to look at our own uniqueness and our own journey. I am a good person because God made all things good. I don't have to run from where I am because this is where God wants me to be. This is where I will meet the God of compassion. My story is important and so is yours. Take time to look at it and reflect upon it. God loves us so much that he always enters the story of our lives.

God is the eternal cherry blossom.

RESTING CATHOLICS

15 January 2012

There was a phrase I liked in a letter I received this week. The writer referred to Catholics 'who are resting'. He explained that actors who are not involved in a current production are never out of work, they are merely 'resting' between jobs.

It's the same for Catholics who can no longer give unqualified support to the present church leadership, he claimed. They are not lost to their religion; they are *resting* from active participation until a church they can identify with returns. They want to be loyal Catholics but find it impossible to stay loyal to the bewildering actions emanating from the power structures of the institutions. Those who are 'resting' will become active again just as soon as leadership shows conscience its due respect.

The managing editor of *The New York Times,* Bill Keller, expressed the same idea forcefully when he described himself as a *collapsed* Catholic. He explained that a 'collapsed Catholic' was someone who was even further removed from the official church than a mere 'lapsed Catholic'.

Collapsed is a good word too. So much of what we once believed and respected is collapsing all around us. The clerical church grows older and, to the average believer, more irrelevant; the image of priesthood has by and large collapsed in the Northern hemisphere. Church attendance has collapsed in urban areas throughout the western world.

The inability of church leadership to discuss the future shape of the church rationally has led to the collapse of life-giving dialogue. As a result respect for the church itself has collapsed and with it the church's credibility. Worst of all, both priests and laity are near a state of collapse from burnout.

What might help to revive our believing community?

It would help greatly if there was a healthy acknowledgement of this state of collapse. To live in denial means certain death. A sincere cry for help, though, works wonders. Bullying, abusing power, attempting to reincarnate the past, and treating mature, educated believers like delinquent children won't work.

What might help restore some pride would be an opportunity to repent humbly and publicly for decades of abuse of children and abuse of power by clergy and religious. An open dialogue which would encourage a sense of community and which would bring hope to people of all faiths and none, would be healing and life-giving. What would help most of all would be a display of Christ-like forgiveness and welcome to the stranger – the central message of the first Eucharist.

We don't need a return to false piety; we need renewal, we need reform. Change is not enough; it is transformation which is essential.

Some say a synod of the Irish church is called for. I'm not enthused. Synod is another of those clerical words which has different meanings for different groups and which has no meaning at all for the laity.

The church still has considerable strengths – not least being those dedicated, educated and deeply-spiritual members who have been purified in the furnace of suffering. Give those lay and clerical members a voice. Respect them and empower them. Allow them to claim a sense of belonging of their church.

In short, instead of trying to impose the Church of Trent on them, resurrect the spirit-filled beauty of the Second Vatican Council on this the Golden Jubilee year of its opening.

THE CRISIS IN IRISH CATHOLICISM

12 August 2012

In a recent article, Robert Kaiser, who was *Time* magazine's religion correspondent at the Second Vatican Council, challenged journalists like me to be positive about the achievements of the Council. Fifty years on, he argued, it's not a wake we're holding.

Rather than grieve for a lost opportunity, we should celebrate what Vatican II has done for us. It has, he insists, given us a new view of ourselves; leaving us free to be human. It has given us a new view of church: 'It's our church, not the pope's church, not the bishop's church, or the priest's church … rather than whine over what daddy wont let us do, we can put the Council into play ourselves.'

That's exactly what Fr Brendan Hoban, a founder member of the Association of Catholic Priests, is attempting to do in his book: *Where do we go from here? The Crisis in Irish Catholicism*. In a selection of twenty readable chapters he charts:

1. Where we are now;
2. What's happening to the Catholic Church in Ireland and;
3. Where do we go from here?

Where we are now is succinctly summed up with a quote from Jesuit priest Peter McVerry: 'The Catholic Church in Ireland is in crisis, a crisis not of our own making, one that is not going to go away. Without root and branch reform, the church, as it currently exists in Ireland, will die – and I will shed no tears. I believe in the church; I have received so much from the church; I believe that the vision of Jesus is vitally important for our time and that the church is the bearer of that vision – but not in its present form.'

Those of us who believed the Council was the work of the Holy Spirit and was the exciting new plan gifted to us by God, willingly dedicated our lives to the cause. As Brendan Hoban writes: 'I certainly didn't go to Maynooth because of the Council but, hand on heart, I would have to say that I probably stayed because of it.'

Now we fear that for thirty years forces who hold the real power within the Catholic Church have frustrated the work of the Council and in doing so have led us into a cul de sac. Hoban believes that had we bought into the Council with enthusiasm and without fear, the church would not be in decline. If we had encouraged the laity to share leadership we could have avoided most of the scandals for which our church is now despised.

'Just to give one example,' he writes. 'If parents were dealing with the allegations of clerical child sex abuse instead of the bishops, the response would have been very different. And the Catholic Church in Ireland might not now be at, what Archbishop Diarmuid Martin famously called, "breaking point". We've paid a high price for not listening to what God said to us in the Spirit driven insights of fifty years ago.'

Brendan Hoban names the real issues whilst answering the vital question as to why the Catholic Church in Ireland is so out of touch with its own people. We need to embrace change to recreate a new and different church: 'A church that listens to itself by listening to its people. A church that loosens the stranglehold of control … and releases the gifts of lay people … a church in tune with the rhythms of our time; a church that cherishes diversity and celebrates difference; a church that names the truth, regardless; a church that implements the teachings of the Second Vatican Council rather than ambushes them along the way' (*Where do we go from here?*, p. 96).

In twenty year's time the Christian churches in Ireland will celebrate 1,600 years since the arrival of St Patrick in AD 432. I wonder what sort of celebrations will take place? What will the state of the Christian churches, especially the Catholic Church, be? I'm sorry I won't be around to experience it.

In his book, *Who Will Break The Bread For Us?*, Fr Brendan Hoban examines this problem and its most obvious symptom – that of disappearing priests. The jacket of his book gives us a strong pictorial image. It's a photograph taken in 1982 of forty-six priests from Brendan Hoban's own diocese of Killala, Co. Mayo, gathered for an annual retreat. There is a reasonable mixture of young and old. The front row however has six aging feeble priests. Fr Hoban writes: 'In less than twenty year's time when we will be celebrating 1,600 years since the coming of St Patrick, present statistics indicate the number of priests in Killala will be the equivalent of the front row of the picture in number and in age. It is not an attractive prospect.'

The question of who will break bread for us is a legitimate one. Fr Hoban continues, 'At most we have a window of a decade or so to come to terms with this crisis. And unless we do, a Eucharistic famine will prevail in Ireland as parishes without Masses will lose their focus and their resilience. Without priests we will have no Mass, without Mass we will have no church … our priests are disappearing and we need to do something about it now.'

The book catalogues the numbers; statistics don't lie. An aging group of burnt-out priests will no longer be able to 'keep the show on the road'. One of his best chapters is entitled 'The Dark'. It's based around Michael Harding's 1986 book *Priest*. It sets the theme magnificently – good but lonely, dysfunctional clergymen fighting a losing battle.

The chapters on celibacy are the most controversial. In turn they look at the arguments for and against compulsory celibacy in the priesthood. Both arguments are fairly treated, yet in a way, both arrive at the same conclusion. If we insist on compulsory celibacy then in less than twenty years from now the priesthood as we know it will have, for all practical purposes, disappeared. If we change to allow married priests, that too will change the church beyond recognition.

Yet there is also a growing tendency within the church to examine whether clericalism rather than celibacy is the issue. We certainly need priests in a Eucharistic church. But does the church have to be built around the present clerical model? That is a question that needs to be teased out more fully than Fr Hoban has the opportunity to do in this book.

Brendan Hoban is a sincere, honest priest who is a focused thinker and brilliant communicator. He is an exceptional talent in the Irish church. I hope he is allowed to continue to write and to challenge us all.

THE DEAD HORSE THEORY

15 January 2012

Now is a good time to drop the blame game and to work for a better future. The past is not a good place to dwell. We can't go on forever flogging a dead horse – which is why I love the insights in this piece, given to me by an enthusiastic teacher.

The tribal wisdom of the Dakota Indians, passed on from generation to generation, says; 'When you discover that you are riding a dead horse, the best strategy is to dismount.'

However in so many parts of society – government, education, religion, etc. – more advanced strategies are often employed, such as:

1. Buying a stronger whip.
2. Changing riders.
3. Appointing a committee to study the horse.
4. Arranging to visit other countries to see how other cultures ride dead horses.
5. Lowering the standards so that dead horses can be included.
6. Reclassifying the dead horse as living-impaired.
7. Hiring outside contractors to ride the dead horse.
8. Harnessing several dead horses together to increase speed.
9. Providing additional funding and / or training to increase the dead horse's performance.
10. Doing a productivity study to see if lighter riders would improve the dead horse's performance.

11. Declaring that as the dead horse does not have to be fed, it is less costly, carries lower overheads and therefore contributes substantially more to the economy than some other horses.
12. Rewriting the expected performance requirements for all horses.

Do I need to say more? I think not!

THE KING JAMES BIBLE

15 May 2011

It is commonly agreed that the most famous Bible ever printed was first published over 400 years ago. The King James Bible first saw the light of day between 2 and 5 May 1611.

The Holy Bible is the most popular book in the world with an estimated six billion copies in circulation. The King James version accounts for one billion of the total. For a translation which was the fruit of forty-seven scholars working over a four-year period, its impact is amazing. For 400 years it has influenced the life and liturgy of countless worshippers in the English-speaking world.

Sir Winston Churchill put it best when he said: 'The scholars who produced this masterpiece are mostly unknown and unremembered. But they forged an enduring link ... between the English-speaking people of the world.'

It's a masterpiece of English prose. Its words and phrases have slipped into common usage. If you 'kill the fatted calf' or 'fight the good fight' you're quoting the King James Bible. Well used clichés like 'sour grapes', 'salt of the earth' and 'feet of clay' come from the same source. You can be your 'brother's keeper', 'cast your pearl before swine' or even be the 'apple of one's eye' and you're unwittingly quoting this 400-year-old translation.

More than 250 unique phrases came to the English language courtesy of the King James Bible. That compares favourably with the great bard, William Shakespeare.

The purpose of the Bible however is to bring us comfort and guidance from God. Here's one of my favourite prayers from the King James Bible, Psalm 23: 'Yea though I walk through the valley of the shadow of death, I will fear no evil; for thou art with me; thy rod and staff, they comfort me.'

What a beautiful image of God!

CORRIE TEN BOOM

16 October 2011

I've been dipping into, *The Hiding Place* which is a story of Corrie ten Boom's amazing life. In the mid-nineteenth century the ten Boom family opened a watch shop in Haarlem in Holland. The family lived in the house above the shop. They were devoted Christians who dedicated their lives to helping their neighbours. Their home was an 'open house' for anyone in need. They were inspired by their faith to serve their church and society as best they could.

During the Second World War the shop was run by Casper ten Boom. Corrie and Betsie were two of his daughters. Their house became a refuge for those hunted by the Nazis. The family knew that if they were caught they would, at the very least, be sent to a concentration camp. But it was their way to practice non-violent resistance against the Nazi oppressors.

During the war there were six or seven people living illegally in their home. Corrie herself became the ringleader within the network in Haarlem and their courageous work meant that at least 800 Jews were saved as well as an unspecified number of Dutch underground workers.

But in February 1944 the family were betrayed and the Gestapo raided their home. Casper, Corrie and Betsie were all arrested as were their uncle Willem, sister Nollie and nephew Peter. The Gestapo searched their house but could not find what they were looking for. They knew that the family were hiding Jewish refugees but they were hidden behind a false wall in Corrie's bedroom. Even though the Nazis kept a continuous watch on the house, the six people escaped and most of them survived the war.

When Casper, who was eighty-four years old was taken to prison, he lived a mere nine days. Corrie and Betsie spent ten months in three different prisons and were eventually brought to the infamous Ravensbruck Concentration Camp near Berlin.

Corrie and Betsie continued to help fellow prisoners. Betsie sadly died in the prison; Corrie was the only one to survive. When she came out she realised that her life was a gift from God and that she would have to live life differently. She wrote, 'There is no pit so deep that God's love is not deeper still … God will give us the love to be able to forgive our enemies.'

In June 1945, after her release from prison at the end of the war, and after the liberation of the Netherlands, Corrie ten Boom felt the need to write one final letter to the person who betrayed her family's work protecting Jews:

Dear Sir,
Today I heard that most probably you are the one who betrayed me. I went through ten months of concentration camp. My father died after nine days of imprisonment. My sister died in prison, too.

The harm you planned was turned into good for me by God. I am nearer to him. A severe punishment is awaiting you. I have prayed for you, that the Lord may accept you if you repent. Think that the Lord Jesus on the cross also took your sins upon himself. If you accept this and want to be his child, you are saved for eternity.

I have forgiven you everything. God will also forgive you everything, if you ask him. He loves you and he himself sent his Son to earth to reconcile your sins. You, on your part, have to give an answer to this. If he says: 'Come unto me, give me your heart,' then your answer must be: 'Yes, Lord, I come, make me your child.' If it is difficult for you to pray, then ask if God will give you his Spirit, who works the faith in your heart. Never doubt the Lord Jesus's love. He is standing with his arms spread out to receive you.

I hope that the path which you will now take may work for your eternal salvation.

Throughout her life she travelled to sixty countries where she testified to God's love. She died on her ninety-first birthday in 1983. Her book *The Hiding Place* has been a bestseller every since.

I love this parable from Corrie's book. It is about a newly-crafted clock which was displayed on a shelf between two old clocks. One of the old clocks ticked ponderously and a little pompously before speaking to the brand new clock.

'I see you have started out in life and I am sorry for you,' he began. 'Just think of what's ahead of you. If you consider how many ticks it takes to tick through a year, you'll never make it. It would have been better if that old man had never wound you up and set your pendulum free.'

So the new clock began to count up the ticks. Each second required two ticks which meant 120 ticks per minute. That amounted to 7,200 ticks per hour, 172,800 ticks per day; in a week the little clock would have to make 1,209,600 ticks for 52 weeks which makes a total of 62,899,200 ticks per year. The new clock fainted on the spot and stopped ticking.

When he came to his senses, he could hear the wise old clock on his other side speaking to him. 'Pay no attention to that old clock,' he said. 'Answer me this: How many ticks have to tick at a time?' 'Only one, I guess,' the new clock answered. 'That's not so hard to do is it? Try it along with me. Just one tick at a time.'

Seventy-five years later the clock was ticking perfectly – one tick at a time.

And Corrie ten Boom draws this conclusion from her parable. No person sinks under the burden of the day. It is only when yesterday's guilt is added to tomorrow's anxiety that our legs buckle and our backs break.

The wisdom of Corrie ten Boom.

🦋 Don't bother to give God instructions; just report for duty.

- Any concern too small to be turned into a prayer is too small to be made into a burden.

- Forgiveness is an act of the will, and the will can function regardless of the temperature of the heart.

- Never be afraid to trust an unknown future to a known God.

- The first step on the way to victory is to recognise the enemy.

- The measure of a life, after all, is not its duration, but its donation.

- When a train goes through a tunnel and it gets dark, you don't throw away the ticket and jump off. You sit still and trust the engineer.

- Worry does not empty tomorrow of its sorrow. It empties today of its strength.

POWER AND AUTHORITY

29 January 2012

I am not sure if many of you saw the excellent programme which Colm Murray did for RTÉ last Monday night. For a Monday night programme it had a huge audience of six hundred thousand. It deserved it.

For those of you who don't know, Colm Murray works in the Sports department of RTÉ and specialises in racing. He's a lovely man in his late fifties and is someone I have great respect for.

Last autumn he revealed on *The Late Late Show* that he was suffering from Motor Neurone Disease (MND). It began with a noticeable limp and then he was diagnosed and was given a few years at most to live.

The documentary picked up on his life last October. By now he is not able to broadcast because his voice has deteriorated and he is permanently in a wheelchair. It was a most moving documentary from a very brave man. It showed that although his body is deteriorating his brain is still sharp. He did the presentation and interviewing for the programme. It was revealed that he was one of a select few taking part in an experiment to find a cure for this dreaded disease. It usually kills people within three years, although there are rare examples of people living longer. Stephen Hawking has been suffering from it for over fifty years. In Hawking's case, although his body is pretty much useless to him now, his brain is still brilliant.

Anyway Colm Murray is working with Professor Orla Hardiman to find a cure. He has taken tablets but he doesn't know if they have a placebo effect or if they are real. He knows that whatever happens it won't help him at all. But he doesn't want to die in vain and the contribution he makes may help to win a cure in the future. In fact Professor Hardiman thinks that there will be a cure within the next fifteen years. Few are as optimistic as the professor.

But it was uplifting to see a brave man suffering from an illness which he called the PITs which means in his mind he's suffering from an illness which is P – for progressive, I – for incurable, T – for terminal.

He gave a wonderful example that even in weakness people can be powerful in the very best sense of the word.

Sadly, Colm Murray passed away on 30 July 2013
and he will be greatly missed!

As it happens, today's gospel is precisely about the distinction between power and authority. A sledgehammer can smash open a nut. It's very powerful. But it doesn't have any respect or authority. It is often said that organisations like the church, wield power but have lost their authority.

If you think of people like Mahatma Gandhi, Martin Luther King, Oscar Romero, they were all influential people, precisely because they identified with the powerless. But through authority they earned respect and changed the lives of those they worked for. It so happened that all three were killed because of the stance they took. The most powerful example of that is Jesus himself. He constantly complained about the Scribes and Pharisees who abused their power and yet had no influence for good at all. He himself was powerless in the material sense, but powerful in the spiritual sense.

There is a wonderful part in today's gospel which puts it brilliantly. Just as great leaders like Gandhi, King and Romero freed people from the demon of oppression, so Jesus freed the man from whatever demons disturbed his life. And the gospel adds, 'His teaching made a deep impression on them, because, unlike the Scribes, he taught them with authority' (Mark 1:22).

I remember Brendan Kennelly, the famous poet, telling me that after he retired from teaching at Trinity College, Dublin, his life was so disrupted that he suffered from depression. He told me that some nights when he couldn't sleep he'd walk the streets from his Dublin city centre apartment. He would walk through Grafton Street and he said he met life at its most raw during those hours. He learned a great deal about himself and about others. He often met street people lying in the shop doors of Grafton Street. Some of them were silent and quiet, others would speak to him. One night he met a young man in a doorway who was obviously disturbed. Another group had robbed this young man of whatever few pence or bottles he had. They had beaten him and when Brendan stopped to speak to him the man slowly and painfully dragged himself up. He recognised Brendan Kennelly and out of the depths he said to him, pointing to the black rings around his eyes, 'These rings are the dark shadows of lost love.' Brendan Kennelly felt humbled before this man. Deep within him he still had beauty. He recognised the poet in Kennelly and he also understood that a poet would recognise the lost poet that was still within him. When everything else was lost, the authority of his art, his giftedness, still survived.

One of John B. Keane's sons explained to me a lesson that he learned from his father, the poet and playwright, on his deathbed. John B. told him that forgiveness was an essential part of life. He went on to outline the three elements to forgiveness:

1. You must never be ashamed to ask for forgiveness if you have done wrong.
2. You must practice and learn to forgive others generously.
3. Be humble enough to forgive yourself.

And John B. Keane then recited the Lord's Prayer. And when he came to the part, 'Forgive us our trespasses ...,' he stopped and told his son, 'It's very important that you recognise that the precept to forgive comes immediately after the phrase, 'Give us this day our daily bread.' Keane recognised that 'our daily bread' is the Eucharist and it is only through the power of the Eucharist that we can experience forgiveness.

Sure You've Loads of Time!

This is the story of three devils who had undergone extensive training on how to lure people into hell.

The master devil had tutored them well and thought them ready to go into the world to search for the lost souls. Before he let them go he asked each of the three devils what their approach would be.

The first said that he would use the classic way. He would convince people that there is no God and therefore they should have a good time without worrying about the consequences.

The second thought he'd have a more philosophical approach. He said he would convince them there was no hell. He reasoned that if God was merciful he wouldn't create a place of torture like hell. There is no hell, so you can enjoy yourself.

The third little devil said he'd use the subtle approach. He'd convince them that there was no hurry. There's plenty of time, live as you are now. Don't change. You'll have plenty of time to convert on your deathbed.

I would say that the last little devil was the one who filled hell.

Charles Schultz

25 September 2011

The following is the philosophy of Charles Schultz, the creator of the *Peanuts* comic strip. You don't need to actually answer the questions. Just think about them. If you read it straight through, you'll get the point:

1. Name the five wealthiest people in the world.
2. Name the last five winners of the Miss World pageant.
3. Name ten people who have won the Nobel or Pulitzer Prize.
4. Name the last five Academy Award winners for best actor and actress.
5. Name the last three winners of the World Cup.

How did you do?

The point is, none of us remembers the headliners of yesterday even though these are no second-rate achievers; they are the best in their fields. Accolades are buried with their owners.

Here's another quiz. See how you do on this one:

1. List two teachers who helped your journey through school.
2. Name three friends who got you through a difficult time.
3. Name five people who have taught you something worthwhile.
4. Think of a few people who have made you feel appreciated and special.
5. Think of five people you enjoy spending time with.

The lesson: The people who make a difference in your life are not the ones with the most money or the most awards. They are the ones who care the most.

CELIBACY

18 September 2011

Bishop Edward Daly's call to end compulsory clerical celibacy hit the headlines on Tuesday last. It amazes me that simple common sense can become a major news story. It's well over thirty years since I called for a discussion about compulsory celibacy for all priests. Back then, I was editorialising in *The Cross* magazine in the early 1970s. *The Irish Press* made a major story of it and it's probably one of the reasons why I've 'a wonderful future behind me'.

Bishop Daly has obviously changed his mind on the issue; if he'd said it was better for Catholic clergy to marry when he was a priest, he'd never have been chosen a bishop. Bishop Brendan Comiskey and Bishop Willie Walsh did make similar sensible statements; Rome spoke and they had to cease speaking. That's the way it happens.

It was interesting to read what one of Bishop Daly's most gifted priests, Denis Bradley, had to say about the issue in *The Irish News*. Denis was a priest in the Derry diocese serving in the Bogside in the 1970s. He fell in love and left the active ministry to marry. 'When I went to the Bishop it was not to say I couldn't live with celibacy,' he told the paper. 'I told him I had two loves – I love the church but I had also fallen in love with somebody. It really was two positives and I had to make a choice.'

Denis chose marriage because he had to, but admits he would return to the priesthood instantly if the rules were modified. In fact no priest could have made the magnificent contribution to the healing of Northern society that Denis Bradley has made in his lifetime. He helped establish Northlands Drug and Alcohol Treatment Centre; he resisted violence and worked for peace with justice; he took on the onerous task of vice-chair of the Policing Board when it was a dangerous position to hold. No priest would have been allowed the freedom. The priesthood lost a shining light, but society gained an even brighter one. Yet Denis still hankers for the priesthood.

The question I was asked most often this week was whether priests would be allowed to marry in my lifetime. Last year I would have answered positively. This year I realise that nothing will change in the immediate future. It will take longer for the Holy Spirit to break through the present system. I won't live that long.

The bottom line is that we already have a married priesthood in the Latin rite. Anglican clergy crossing over to the Roman church are ordained Roman Catholic priests and are free to live fully as married priests in the Catholic Church. That means there is absolutely no principle involved here. It's simply an unwillingness, or an inability, to change.

What we need is for active bishops and priests across the world to end their 'prudent' silence and speak out as the retired bishop of Derry has. The majority of priests and bishops are in favour of a married priesthood because it would undoubtedly add to the quality of the priesthood. Sadly fear rules because few want to put their heads above the parapet. Except of course those who believe in integrity of life and those with nothing much to lose.

VOCATIONS

26 April 2010

Today is Vocation Sunday and Good Shepherd Sunday. The fourth Sunday after Easter is always Good Shepherd Sunday because there is an extract from the gospel each year written by St John which explains a little bit more about how the Lord is the Good Shepherd and will stay with us until the end of time. When you read over the gospel again, you will see that Jesus said that his people belonged to him, they listen to his voice, he knows them, they follow him and he will give them eternal life and they will never be lost. These are most consoling words and we need to hear them.

It reminds me of the story of the revivalist tent meeting in a gospel hall. The preacher was having a healing session one night. And at the end of it he asked, if there is anyone who wants to be prayed over individually let them come to the front of the church. So John joined the queue in a modest and quiet way and when he reached the front the preacher said to him, 'What do you want me to pray for?' And John says, 'I want you to pray for my hearing.' So the preacher laid his hands on John's head, put them over his ears, clasped his ears. He put his finger into John's ears and asked the Lord that they be cleared and the Lord grant him hearing. The preacher said, 'Now John, has the Lord done anything for your hearing?' To which John replied, 'I don't know sir because my hearing is not until next Wednesday.' Sometimes we listen but don't hear.

I want to share with you a little piece which I got great succour from during the week: 'I have lived unhappily through some of the recent public controversies over church-based scandals and disputes. I have been saddened, disappointed, angered, shocked and frustrated, sometimes all in the one day. But what has it meant for me, for my faith in God and my faith in church? My faith in Christ and in the church has to be precisely that – *mine* – felt deeply in my own life and in my own soul, linked to Christ and to the church only. If my faith is strong only for as long as no priest commits a crime, no bishop makes a mistake, no member of the church is hypocritical or sinful, then was it ever faith in the first place? If my faith shatters because someone whom I respect or admire turns out to be a public sinner, who then was my guide? Was it Jesus Christ, or was it merely a very human understudy?' That was President Mary McAleese.

A good shepherd will never let us down. We put our faith in the shepherd, not in the hireling.

During the week I went to Omagh CBS for a Vocations Day seminar. There were 110 lads broken into small groups. My group asked me why I became a priest. I told them it started in a confessional box fifty years ago when a priest asked if I wanted to become a priest and I said no and he said you should think about it. Fifty years later here I am on this altar. I have no idea how I arrived at this point, but I know that's where it started. I explained all that to the pupils and they asked what it was like to be a priest.

We had a great discussion about it. I asked them what they thought of priests. They knew that:

1. Priests worked very hard.
2. That they are getting old all the time.
3. That often they kept too much control of things in the parish.
4. They were out of touch with their lives and indeed most priests were so old they were out of touch with their parent's lives too.
5. They were against celibacy. One of the boys couldn't think of the word. So he said, what's that thing where you can't marry and another said it was a blessing. So I explained it was celibacy. They didn't see any sense at all in that.
6. They didn't see why we should be a priest for life. They said they'd be willing to give a few years of their life, the same as they do when going to foreign lands with Concern or Goal. But they said there is no job for life now so why should this be for life.

I thought it was terrific. They had a real sense of where the church is going. There was no anger. It was just that our system was out of touch with theirs. I went into it reluctantly but came out of it enthused. I'd love to be starting off again. Because I think the church of the future will be better, healthier and I'd feel more at home in it than in the church of the present.

Maya Angelou's poem says it all:

> People will forget what you said;
> People will even forget what you did;
> But people will never forget how you made them feel.

That's vocation!

THE PASTOR'S ASS

September 2011

The pastor entered his donkey in a race and it won. The pastor was so pleased with the donkey that he entered it in another race again and it won again. The local paper read:

PASTOR'S ASS OUT FRONT.

The bishop was so upset with this kind of publicity that he ordered the pastor not to enter the donkey in another race. The next day the headline read:

BISHOP SCRATCHES PASTOR'S ASS.

This was too much for the bishop so he ordered the pastor to get rid of the donkey. The pastor decided to give it to a nun in a nearby convent. The local paper, hearing of the news, posted the following headline:

NUN HAS BEST ASS IN TOWN.

The bishop fainted. He informed the nun that she would have to get rid of the donkey so she sold it to a farmer for £10. The next day the paper read:

NUN SELLS ASS FOR £10.

This was too much for the bishop so he ordered the nun to buy back the donkey and lead it to the hills where it could run wild. The next day the headlines read:

NUN ANNOUNCES HER ASS IS WILD AND FREE.

The bishop was buried two days later.

The moral of the story is … being concerned about public opinion can bring you much grief and misery … even shorten your life. So be yourself and enjoy life!

Stop worrying about everyone else's ass and you'll be a lot happier and live longer!

ABANDONING RELIGION

19 August 2012

A survey of one thousand people in Ireland concluded that Irish people are abandoning religion at an alarming rate. The same questions were put, online, to samples of one thousand people in fifty-one countries. The result in Ireland was that only 47% of Irish people declared themselves to be 'a religious person'. In 2005, when the last survey was carried out, that figure was 69%.

The result seems puzzling. The most recent census had 84% of people categorising themselves as Catholic. Yet an Amárach Survey carried out for the Association of Catholic Priests (whose sample was also one thousand people) showed that Irish people have a strong spiritual foundation but find it difficult to accept some core teachings and practices of the Catholic Church.

In the national census only 5% said they had no religion whilst in this survey 10% claimed to be atheists.

I wouldn't argue with the prevailing trend of the survey, namely that there is a growing number of people who are disillusioned with religion. I don't believe however that they have no religion or that they are not spiritual people.

The way the question was framed, and the time at which the survey took place, had a bearing on its outcome. Firstly since 2005 there has been a series of reports whose conclusions were damning for leadership in the Catholic Church. Secondly, just because people say they are 'not religious' does not mean they have abandoned their relationship with God. Many have a personal relationship with God and a mature spirituality even though they wouldn't admit to being 'religious'. To be religious, in some circumstances, means the person is 'a holy Joe'. I believe there are far more people interested in religion and in leading a good life than this survey allows.

Katie Taylor's strong expression of faith will give many young people the courage to admit they need to have a relationship with God even though most Christian churches are not providing a suitable outlet for their spirituality.

The most pressing challenge facing all religions now is to find the key to being relevant in people's lives. Worldwide studies indicate that young people, when they reach the age of fifteen, want to disconnect themselves from the church. For many it becomes a permanent withdrawal but for others it's a time of searching which often leads to them returning with an even stronger faith.

Leaving the church has become an easy option. And since the churches rarely make much of an effort to find out why people leave, they frequently end up drifting through life disconnected from the religion of their youth and unsure of their relationship with God.

We need to seek the lost sheep with compassion and with enthusiasm. From the letters I receive I see some trends. First of all, churches don't seem interested in accommodating younger people with their doubts. The feeling, from those who have written to me, is that the church claims to have all the answers. Christian churches are said to demonise anything with which they don't agree.

Our task is to find ways of listening to and speaking with people who no longer feel comfortable within church. We don't have all the answers; there is no point pretending we do.

Furthermore most young people find the church's view on sex and sexuality mystifying. The church's views on sexual practice are so far removed from their life experience that there is precious little common ground left. The now generation is comfortable with their own practice and feels rejected and harshly judged by the church. We need to talk if the church is to communicate its teachings and values.

The result is that the church is not a place they go to find answers about life. That's the 'new normal'. And the church has lost it relevance and its voice in this 'new normal'.

We have to be enthusiastic about reaching out to people who disagree with us. We must identify with people's worries and be able to appreciate them in a respectful way. Religion is not irrelevant. As Pope Benedict wrote: 'To listen to the concerns of young people … is not merely something expedient; it represents a primary duty for society as a whole, for the sake of building a future of justice and peace.'

OLIVIA O'LEARY

8 January 2012

I haven't spoken with Olivia O'Leary in a long time; but I've listened to her, and learned from her, with ever-increasing appreciation. Olivia is first of all a wise, sensible person, she's a real journalist with reasoned opinions which you accept or reject and feel equally enlightened either way. Furthermore Olivia O'Leary can be radical in the truest meaning of the word – she gets to the root of the problem. And she's fair. She gives credit where credit is due and occasionally even when it isn't due. She is more than fair. That's why her assertion on RTÉ's *Drivetime* that she had left the Catholic Church saddened me; it didn't shock me, it just knocked the stuffing out of me in the month of Christmas.

If a cultured, professional, impartial woman like Olivia O'Leary can no longer feel welcome in the Catholic Church, what hope is there? It's precisely people like her that the Catholic Church needs in its midst and needs to listen to. She said that it was the Catholic Church's refusal to ordain women which was the main reason, though the institutional cover-up of clerical child sexual abuse was also an 'approximate factor'.

She didn't leave with a sense of triumph, but heartfelt regret, because she has uncles and aunts who are priests and nuns and many friends whom she respects greatly. These are decent, good, generous people. But the dictates of the leaders give the impression of being out of touch with any known, real, world.

Olivia said, 'No longer at my age can I accept a subordinate role; not for myself, not for my daughter, not for my sisters, my nieces or friends.'

Like all of us, she kept on hoping things would change, but when she heard the voice of the traditional male church, in the form of author George Weigel give, 'the same old non-reasons for the refusal of the church to ordain women – we have different tasks, different gifts … God made men and women different for a reason,' she realised nothing will change.

Again, like so many others, Olivia doesn't feel rage, so much as weariness. 'Difference is still latched onto as a reason to discriminate; weariness, and, for me, relief, that it's all over now. I have moved on out,' she reasoned.

She will of course miss 'the liturgy, one of the world's great art forms and such a comfort at times of loss and pain'. She'll also miss family and friends, but realises that, 'it is their humanity that distinguishes them, not their role in an institution and it is our humanity which distinguishes us, not the fact that we are women.'

For the present she will worship with the Church of Ireland and anyway she'll 'celebrate by simply being outside in the wind and the rain, outside in the sunshine, walking the world that the creator made for us all equally. Not because we are male or female but because we are human,' she concluded.

We can agree or disagree, but we ignore the challenge Olivia offers at our peril.

Recently I've been thinking that church leadership is so out of touch largely because time and energy is directed to dealing with the fallout from the abuse issue as well as protecting the institution itself.

Shoring up the institution and protecting children are both necessary roles, but what's lacking is time and energy to listen to the genuine concerns of so many weary priests and people alike.

Genuinely good leaders find themselves dealing with the fallout of sexual abuse day and night. It has become impossible for leaders, even if they wanted to, to deal with the equally urgent problems facing the church everywhere. It's one of the unseen results of the evil that is sexual abuse. So much energy is focused on finding a solution to that awful problem, and to removing those responsible for it from ministry, that there is little energy left to plan for genuine spiritual renewal. The leaders are right to protect children and remove the cancer of sexual abuse from the body of the church. But sooner or later the fact that decent, good, honourable and spiritual people like Olivia O Leary, are marching out of the Catholic Church has to be acknowledged. Will there be anything worthwhile left when the evil of sex abuse is finally dealt with? That's the question.

BLUEBELLS

29 April 2012

This is the first Sunday after news was revealed that Fr Brian was censured by the Congregation for the Doctrine of Faith in March 2011.

I begin by thanking you for your support when the news broke on Thursday. Since then it has been hectic and there have been hundreds of phone calls, texts, emails and letters. There is absolutely no possibility that I will be able to reply to them all. So I would ask you to take this as an acknowledgement and thanks of your very precious support.

I don't want to bring my difficulties with the Vatican into your lives today. You have a perfect right to come to Mass and not to be assaulted with my problems. So I'll try not to speak too much about it though of course it is very much on my mind.

I apologise to you that I wasn't able to tell you about my position until now. It was just not possible to do so because of the way the censure was passed down from our general in Rome to our provincial and then to me.

Many of us are angry today and that's a fitting response to what happened. But we must not let our anger at part of the leadership of the church have an effect on our relationship with God. We have to make choices for ourselves; faith is a personal gift from God to each of us and each of us must respond in a personal way. But thank you for your support, prayers, presence and most of all your hugs.

Do you remember I mentioned last week the sin I committed as a novice when I was ordered by the rector to cut down twenty beautiful cherry trees. I obeyed blindly and did as I was told. But

I now know that even though I obeyed blindly, my choice was morally wrong. I didn't realise it would be so relevant this week. Sometimes obedience to the letter of the law is not the best or even a good moral choice. Doing 'the right thing' is not the same as 'doing what is right'.

I am still with nature this week. On Friday after a very tough day in Belfast I came home and Pat Lunny, a friend and local photographer, reminded me that the bluebells were out on Innis Davar. When I got there I discovered that perhaps there weren't as many bluebells as there were last year. Well not yet anyway. The grass seemed to have been able to grow faster than the bluebells during what is a cold spring.

At first I was slightly disappointed but then I realised I was missing the beauty of special gifts from God by concentrating on the absent bluebells. By concentrating negatively I failed to enjoy the magnificence of God's special gift to me. From that moment on as I wandered around the twenty-acre island on a cold Friday evening I became more in tune with nature.

I watched the trees and some of them were beautifully dressed in forty shades of green whilst others were naked and maybe in some cases dead. Yet when the birds sang on the naked trees I could see them. As I learned last year, a bird can still bring life to a dead tree.

I then went over the edge of the lake and spotted ten swans spread out on a choppy lake. I was amazed at how uncomfortable the swans were. Their necks instead of being S-shaped were straight up. They were trying to balance on the babbling waves. They were far from their normal peaceful selves but as by instinct, when they sensed that I was on the shore, they came together in a straight line. It's probably their instinct to protect one another. But something happened them too when they moved close together, they seemed to regain control. Their necks went into the beautiful balanced relaxed S-shape. Their bodies were in perfect harmony with the rocky waters. Together they had overcome the storm. When they were separated and lost, the storm was in control of them.

I learned a lesson from the swans. We must stick together. Your encouragement helps me overcome the storms of life too. I watched the swans for a long time and as this community of supportive swans became a picture of peace and contentment. As I wandered back across the island I notice that there was a quarter moon in the sky even though the sun was still shining. Almost on cue the sun began to drop. By the time I reached the waters edge it was like liquefied gold melting into its watery bed. I knew that the sun would rise tomorrow as it has done for thousands of years in that same spot. The bluebells, the grass, the trees naked and clothed, the swans, the birds singing. Nobody can bottle the beauty of God and nobody has a monopoly on it either. That's what gave me strength to have a restful mind as I went to Marian Finucane for the interview yesterday. God cannot be confined to our human minds. God's compassion can not be imprisoned in laws, state or church. God is eternal and has loved the unlovable before any church claimed an exclusive franchise on God's love.

The story of the Good Shepherd is apt when we pray, especially for vocations. It was unusual that Jesus should call himself a shepherd. Shepherds were not highly respected individuals. They were not trustworthy people. And yet Jesus seemed to identify with shepherds even from his birth.

When the Son of God was born in a lonely cave, it was the lonely shepherds who came to visit him. It was another surprise when he said he was the good shepherd. Shepherds looked after thousands of sheep from March to November on high ground. They were ruthless in protecting their sheep. It was their livelihood and they had to protect them from hyenas, jackals, wolves and robbers. They did it with knives and any other weapon that could stop robbers stealing their sheep. Shepherds walked in front of their flocks and knew the name of each sheep. At night they lay across the gateway or door of the pen in which the sheep rested to keep the robbers out. Jesus compares himself to a good shepherd. He considers his life to be less important than the flock. Jesus, during his life, shows that he is a good shepherd who confronts his oppressors face to face. He won't let anyone harm the little ones. Jesus went before his people to suffer for them and to save them. Jesus laid down his life and went out of his way to find the lost sheep. And our vocation is to love like Jesus and to be as selfless as the good shepherd.

C. S. Lewis said that vocation could be summed up with four calls to love.

1. The call to love in marriage and family.
2. The call to love in a dedicated and exclusive way. This is the religious life where attachments are given up and one dedicates ones life to God.
3. Sometimes there is a vocation to love as a single person. To lead one's single life in a dedicated selfless way.
4. The call to the ordained ministry.

All of them are important. And all vocations are based around the four C's. *Care, Compassion, Charity* and a willingness to accept a *Cause* greater than our own egos.

Sometimes we as individuals are the Good Shepherd; at other times we are the sheep in need of care. Sometimes we are the shepherds who reach out to the lost and lonely. At other times we are the sheep in need of the shepherd's guiding hand.

The gospel says that the shepherd must be willing to 'lay down' his life for his sheep. The word lay down is the same phrase that is used on Holy Thursday when Jesus lays aside and lays down his garment and washes feet to indicate a ministry of service.

In the Acts of the Apostles the newly-baptised Christians were asked to lay aside their processions so that the more deserving members of the community could be helped. The broken, the rejected, the exiled, the excluded, the condemned, the pushed aside, those on the edge, are all drawn back to the centre through Jesus. Jesus says, 'I have other sheep that do not belong ... I must lead them too.' Maybe it's best summed up in what Pierre Teilhard de Chardin once said. He himself was a Christian philosopher who was regarded with suspicion by his own church because of some of his significant writings. But when John XXIII called the Council he was brought back into the fold and journeyed to the centre. No wonder he could say, 'Love is the only force that can make things one without destroying them.'

GOOD LEADERS

11 March 2012

Leaders are important. Research shows that a project or a company with a good leader will be 15% more successful because of the leader. Conversely a bad leader will have a minus effect of 15%. So the difference between a good leader and a bad leader in a community could be as much as 30%. That's why the corporate world will go to any lengths to get the right leader and will pay any price to ensure he or she stays. One person really does have far-reaching effects.

Recent research showed that the essential characteristic of a good leader is that they know and understand their own strengths. They are clear about what they bring to a specific role. They can discern those who work with, and those who work against, them. They have no hesitation in hiring and firing to make their plans work.

That same research shows that the vast majority of people have the potential to be an effective leader once they find their proper niche.

Another characteristic of good leaders is that they have the ability to solve problems. They recognise a problem, they think about it and listen for solutions. Then they have the ability to pick the right course of action.

Good leaders have a way of listening to everyone and not just the most vocal. They recognise who has the best ideas. Often it's the quietest person in the room who has the most practical insights which they will share, given the opportunity.

Good leaders know their limits. They make sure not to be promoted beyond their abilities.

Good leaders are quick to spot conflict and know how to nip it in the bud. Too often the first effect of conflict is that one person is demonised. This is fatal when you're building a team. Troublemakers make demons of others and martyrs of themselves.

Those who feed feelings of rejection become so self-centred that they interpret every difference of opinion as a personal rejection. Before long the self-proclaimed victim provokes and even creates situations where they are rejected. In short people who see themselves as hard done by create a fantasy world in which most of their colleagues are perceived to be working against them.

A good leader will convince the disturbed person to admit that the others in the team are not monsters. They are people you can listen to and respect, even if you can't always agree with them.

A bad leader not only avoids conflict, but doesn't even acknowledge it. A bad leader lives in denial. Avoiding the problem allows feelings to fester and the problem quickly becomes unsolvable because trust and respect disappear.

The psychologist Doug Stone perfected 'the third story,' approach to conflict. For Stone 'the first story' is my view of the issue. I'm right and you're wrong. 'The second story' is the other person's view where they are right and I am wrong. 'The third story' is a way of setting up a conversation so that the problem is described in such a way that both of us can agree it is accurate. It's recognising that difference doesn't have to lead to conflict.

Stone also discovered that you can't have a good exchange of views if one person is always the good talker and the other the good listener. People have to share how they experience things. Everyone must listen and speak respectfully and honestly.

Eventually good leaders recognise that some conflicts can't be solved yet they cannot be allowed to frustrate the teams' mission. In the last analysis it's a choice between accepting the solution or walking away.

No matter how important people are in a team, they cannot be allowed to poison the project.

It's no wonder good leaders are cherished.

DULL SERMONS

21 August 2011

I've been enjoying a book which I don't think is available here, called *101 Things To Do During A Dull Sermon*. It's a 'survival guide for sermon victims. 'Rather than yawn, have a laugh' is their motto. The suggestion I liked best for coping with a dull sermons is this one:

'Devise ways of climbing into the balcony without using the stairs.' Do that in some other church please.

Another mad suggestion to pass away the time during a dull sermon is this: 'When one baby in an otherwise silent congregation begins to cry loudly, other babies will often join in. By getting the baby nearest you to start crying (take away his dummy, make ugly faces, etc.) see how many other babies you can get to cry all at the same time. Count the babies crying and compare with a number that a friend can make cry during the next dull sermon. Highest number wins. Some bonus points if you can make the preacher cry.'

Here's another one you might find helpful: 'Since many people in your congregation only work a five-day week, devise a suitable list of jobs for the sixth day and submit it to them after church. Job ideas might include ironing the vicar's poodle or dry-cleaning the organist's toupee.' That might actually be more dangerous than scaling a rope into the balcony.

Speaking of toupees this one amuses me. 'The hairs on your head are numbered, yes. But do you know the number? Try counting them during the sermon. If there are too many to count on one Sunday, divide it up and count only those hairs on one side of your parting. A variation on this activity, suitable for upper-middleclass congregations, is to count the number of toupees.'

This next suggestion happens more frequently than you think. It's called the misplaced Amen. 'Shout a loud, "Amen" at the conclusion of a sentence that isn't particularly inspiring. Wait and see if anyone else chimes in with, "Amen," or if the sermon suddenly becomes lively in response to your response.'

I'd say this one has been tried before: 'Compose a letter to your preacher extolling the spiritual rewards to be had on a solitary camping exhibition. Then offer to lend him your camping gear if he will take a few weeks off.' I'd nearly preach a dull sermon myself just to get a break.

At the moment I am trying to make our church more comfortable so I particularly enjoyed this one: 'By experimentation, try to determine how many comfortable pew sitting positions you can discover. (You will kill a lot of time before you realise there are no comfortable pew sitting positions.)'

I love off-the-wall ideas. And this one, known as the fake head trick, is surely off-the-wall: 'During the week take some time to sculpt and paint an exact likeness of your head. Within the church wear the fake head on top of your shoulders. Your real head will be down inside your jacket and you will be free to sleep, or if you bring a flashlight you can read the Sunday paper. If you are a particularly clever artist you may want to try the "fake head and body trick" which would leave you free to enjoy a coffee in town.'

Too many people are already trying the 'smelly sock solution'. 'Refrain from washing your socks for eleven days. During the sermon remove your shoes. Warning. Don't bother if your minister hasn't yet received the gift of smell.'

This one is funny: 'Slap your neighbour. See if he or she turns the other cheek. If not raise your hand and tell the Pastor.'

Cue cards are all the rage these days, but I am not looking forward to seeing these ones in our church: 'Help the preacher by giving him a responsive audience. From the pew hold up large cards that will help the congregation to respond in unison … sample cards: 'Amen.' 'I hear you.' 'That's right,' 'Ha ha ha …' but on the other hand you could use cards, designed to help the preacher keep in touch with the moods of the audience. Sample cards this time: 'Get to the point,' 'Tell another joke,' 'You're fading fast,' 'We're praying for you.'

Maybe we are not as boring as we think. As a final suggestion the authors have this comforting comparison: 'List some things that would be even more boring than listening to a dull sermon. For example a) writing this year's Christmas list. b) Balancing your bank account. c) Cleaning your comb. d) Humming an Andy Williams tune.'

These summer days I thought *101 Things To Do During A Dull Sermon* might entice you to go back to church.

HOPE

1 April 2012

The American novelist, Nigel Hawthorne, once said: 'Happiness is like a butterfly, which, when pursued, is just beyond your grasp, but which, if you sit quietly will alight upon you.' Like all helpful insights, it takes time and reflection to uncover its wisdom.

In my work as a priest I often meet heroism and holiness where I least expect it. I'm thinking of a young man I knew who, in the prime of his life, was told he was suffering from a terminal illness. At the time, he and his wife were blissfully happy, looking forward to starting their family. I dreaded going to see them when they asked me to chat through the funeral arrangements. It wasn't that long since I'd helped plan their wedding. On the long drive through Ireland towards their house, I prayed a lot and rehearsed words of comfort over and over in my head.

To my surprise the young man and his wife were by now much further along the road to emotional healing than I was. When I stumbled through half-baked expressions of sorrow, the man, though spent and weak, clasped his wife's hand and said: 'Brian you know there are worse things then dying.'

When I asked what could be worse than dying, he replied: 'To live to old age and never know the love we have.' When it came to his funeral Mass I told that story; it was all anyone there remembered – and it was all they needed to remember.

We never know what we're capable of until we're pushed. Michelangelo could sculpt a beautiful, delicate, warm, protective angel out of a hard, cold slab of marble. He was once asked to explain his technique for that particular work of art. His answer was brilliant: 'I looked at the marble block and saw an angel there. I worked diligently until I set the angel free.'

That gives me hope. If I look long enough at my own cold heart, I'll discover the angel of happiness waiting to be set free.

COPING WITH ADVERSITY

5 February 2012

You have often heard the phrase, 'Job's comforter'. Well Job's story is about a continuous struggle with God. The Book of Job is how we cope when things go wrong in life. To the outside world Job was the perfect man. He had a good farm, plenty of money, a good wife. He had seven sons and three daughters. If you wanted a good neighbour then you couldn't get a better one than Job because he helped everyone.

But then quite suddenly he lost his farm and most of his money. His family fell apart. His health was poor and his world collapsed. He had nobody to turn to. No matter how he prayed, nothing changed. So he spoke to his wife and she told him that since he had prayed to God, God had let him down. The best thing he could do now was to curse God and see who would help him. And that's what a 'Job's comforter' is; it gives you advice that is not much good to you.

So Job decided to pray about it and that's what he is doing when we meet him in today's reading. 'It seems as if my whole life is nothing but pure drudgery. I am like a slave who will never get paid. I can't even sleep at night. When I am lying in bed I can't wait for morning to come and when I get up I can't wait for night to come.' He's obviously in a bad way. But if you read Job more deeply you will begin to see that when he concludes, 'My life is but a breath,' it is really helpful to him. He recognises that everything fell apart suddenly, but in God's world everything can come together just as suddenly if we have faith. In another place he says, 'The Lord gives; the Lord takes away; blessed be the name of the Lord.' In good times and in bad times God is with us if we can only see where God is leading us. Job went on. 'I trusted in God in the good times so I must learn to trust him in the bad times too.' That's Job's story.

Paul is also a man with a story to tell. He's experienced God in bad times too. He's been in prison, he has suffered lashings, he's been shipwrecked. He's been rejected and left without money all on account of the gospel. Today he has come to the conclusion that this is part of what preaching the gospel entails. He'll do anything to make it work. 'I make myself a slave of everyone's, so as to win as many as I can … I made myself all things to all men in order to save some at any cost.' Another great act of faith in God.

Jesus in the gospel comes with a story to tell too. Mark's gospel begins with Jesus curing people and selecting followers at a ferocious pace. Today we find him at the home of Peter's mother-in-law who is sick. You don't need me to point out that if Peter had a mother-in-law, he must have had a wife. And don't forget Peter was not just a priest but was the first pope. So no matter what people say, Jesus had no trouble at all with married priests or indeed married popes. It is interesting what happens. Jesus greets her, takes her by the hand, then he heals her and she immediately serves food. In fact and this is an interesting point too, a woman, Peter's mother-in-law, becomes as it were his fifth disciple in the order Mark has them listed here.

Jesus himself was facing an inner struggle as well with loneliness and we should note how he faced it. The gospel tells us that he walked to a lonely place. In other words he walked towards loneliness; he didn't run away from it.

Itzhak Perlman was inflicted with Polio at an early age but became a famous violinist even though he suffered from the effects of the disease all his life. He had to wear callipers. One night he was giving a concert with a famous orchestra. With great difficulty he walked on to the stage, clicked his callipers, sat down and began to play the violin. It was a complicated classical piece. Early on, one of the strings on his violin broke. And for the rest of the piece he struggled to play this complicated piece on three strings. Nobody said that he did it well, but he did do it on three strings. Somebody asked him afterwards why he didn't stop the whole proceedings and have the string replaced. His answer was brilliant: 'Sometimes you have to find out how much music you can make with what you are left with.' That's a wonderful example and summary of the gospel and life itself. Make the best of the hand you are dealt.

Choosing the Twelve Apostles

16 September 2012

Companies screen people for management positions and church authorities also screen candidates for the priesthood.

Imagine that the twelve apostles were sent by Jesus to a firm of consultants for similar tests. This might well be the report he'd receive.

Thank you for submitting the resumes of the twelve men you have picked for management positions in your new organisation. All of them have now taken our battery of tests. We have run the results through our computer, and also arranged personal interviews for each of them with our psychologists and vocational aptitude consultants. The results of all the tests are included, and we advise that you study them carefully.

It is the opinion of the staff that most of your nominees are lacking in education and vocational aptitude for the type of enterprise you are undertaking. We have found evidence of jealousy and rivalry among them. Therefore, we would recommend that you should continue your search for persons of experience and proven ability.

附 *Simon Peter is emotionally unstable and given to fits of temper. He is definitely not the man you would want to head your organisation.*

附 *Andrew and Philip have absolutely no qualities of leadership – they are followers.*

附 *The two brothers, James and John, are too hot-headed. Besides, they place personal interest above company loyalty.*

ᬄ *Thomas demonstrates a questioning attitude which will undermine morale.*

ᬄ *Matthew, the tax-collector, is undoubtedly a man of ability, but would project the wrong image for an organisation such as yours.*

ᬄ *James (son of Alphaeus), Thaddaeus and Simon (called 'the Zealot') have radical leanings. Hence, their unsuitability.*

ᬄ *Bartholomew is nondescript.*

ᬄ *There is one of the candidates, however, who shows potential. He is a man of ability and resourcefulness, good with people, has a keen business mind, and has contacts in high places. He is highly motivated, ambitious and responsible. That man is Judas Iscariot. We recommend him as your controller and leader.*

We wish you every success in your new venture.

Sincerely yours,
Jordan Management Consultants

With thanks to whoever it was who first composed this insightful report.

TEN CHARACTERISTICS OF GOOD LEADERS

Yale University once came up with a long list of characteristics, believed to be common to all Good Leaders.

People like lists of ten so I've done my own list:

A Good Leader

1. They have a high level of tolerance. Good leaders can hold their feelings in check. They don't allow their feelings to interfere with their ability to work.

2. They encourage others to participate. In reaching decisions, they welcome the input of others and yet are not paralysed by too much information.

3. They continually question their motives and their methods. They look for flaws in their thinking but are not upset by mistakes. They try to understand their own prejudices.

4. They are competitive. They realise that other people are out to beat them and they enter into the competition without personal hostility.

5. They keep impulses to 'get even' under control. Others will be hostile. It's part of the process. They don't take it personally. They keep their cool.

6. They win quietly. They are excited when they achieve; they feel good about it but don't get carried away.

7. They lose graciously – in public anyway. They keep perspective. A setback is not an excuse to give up.

8. They recognise genuine restrictions. Law and life both impose restrictions. It's part of the equation.

9. They are conscious of loyalties. They are loyal to their friends, their co-workers, their management, and their personal and close friends. Loyalty is the difference between a good leader and a great leader.

10. They set realistic goals. The bar is high enough to make them fight to achieve, but sensible enough to be achievable.

How many of them have you got? How can you improve?

OSCAR ROMERO

4 April 2010

Oscar Romero was Archbishop of San Salvador for just three years. When he was appointed in 1977 he was known as a pious, conservative bishop who wouldn't rock the boat. He changed completely when his friend Rutilio Grande a Jesuit priest, was murdered because of his commitment to the poor. His friend's death transformed Romero from a timid, conventional cleric to an outspoken champion of justice. On 24 March 1980 Archbishop Romero was assassinated by a single shot through the heart as he offered Mass. He was the first bishop to be murdered at the altar since Thomas Beckett in the twelfth century.

In his weekly broadcast sermons, Romero highlighted social injustices, stood up for the poor and denounced corrupt leaders.

'We either serve the life of Salvadorans or we are accomplices in their death,' he said. 'We either believe in a God of life or we serve the idols of death,' was his simple philosophy. He was accused by his fellow bishops and the ruling elite of subordinating the gospel to politics. But Romero answered by pointing to the courage of the poor and saying, 'With these people it is not hard to be the good shepherd.'

On the day before his death he appealed to Salvadoran soldiers to disobey illegal orders. 'We are your people,' he said. 'The peasants you kill are your own brothers and sisters. When you hear the voice of a man commanding you to kill, remember instead the voice of God. 'Thou shalt not kill.'

The next day as he was offering Mass, a single rifle shot was fired from the rear of the church. Romero was struck in the heart and died within minutes.

He was immediately acclaimed a martyr and a saint by the people. In an interview two weeks before the assassination he clearly anticipated his death. He said, 'I have frequently been threatened with death. I must say that as a Christian I do not believe in death but in the resurrection. If they kill me, I shall rise again in the Salvadoran people ... A bishop will die but the church – the people of God will never die.'

And that is why Oscar Romero will be remembered in ceremonies this week on every continent in the world, as one of the few genuine martyrs in modern times. As he said himself, 'I rejoice that we are persecuted whilst being the voice of the poor. ... How sad it would be in a country where such horrible murders have been committed if there were no priests among the victims.' At the time there were 75,000 Salvadorans killed and one million fled the country.

That is how we should remember Romero – by standing up to injustice big or small wherever we meet it.

OUR IMAGE OF GOD

18 March 2012

It has been said that religion is for those who fear hell whilst spirituality is for those who have already been there. Sometimes religion invents a God that becomes the justification for what people want themselves. Religions often use God to bring about what they want. As Gay Byrne mentioned during his talk in The Graan at the novena of hope, it's a pity the Commandments are written in, 'Thou shall not,' formula. Actually when we look at them the Commandments are aids to good living. It's only when they are expressed in negative commands that we object to them.

But the readings today make a completely different point. Could you imagine God saying to you at this moment, 'You are a work of art'? Yet that's exactly what God says to us in Ephesians (2:4–10): 'You are God's work of art created in Christ Jesus to live the good life … God loved with so much love that he was generous with his mercy.' Then we come to the gospel itself. Every sporting event has a quotation from today's gospel on a placard nearest the scoring zones. John 3:16 is the most familiar text in the sporting world. And listen to what it says. 'God loved the world so much that he gave his only son, so that everyone who believes in him may not be lost, but may have eternal life.' That's a wonderful promise from God. That's why we are God's work of art.

Mostly though religion, and our own image of God, makes it impossible for us to see ourselves as a work of art forever loved by God. Gerard Hughes, in his book, *The God of Surprises,* tells us about the image of God that many of us have which distorts the true meaning of God.

He had been a university chaplain. He noticed that many of the students, as soon as they came to university, disappeared from the church forsaking the practice of their religion. He wondered why. He asked some of them to describe their image of God. In the process he composed a composite picture of God. He imagined it in this way. A father and mother gather up their two young children each Sunday. They dress them up and put them in the back seat of the car. They explain to the children that they are going to visit good old Uncle George. Uncle George is a rich uncle. He has everything you could ask for in this world. The parents insist he's an extremely nice and helpful uncle. When the children visit him they are instructed to make sure they behave in a proper fashion. They must do nothing out of the ordinary. Uncle George must be placated, Uncle George must be pleased at all costs. When the parents arrive at the big house where Uncle George lives, they are brought into a perfectly positioned room. The parents once again remind them not to do anything that would upset uncle George.

Uncle George came in and was kind to the children. But then he brings them down to the basement where there is a huge furnace. As the kids approach the furnace they can hear screams and crying coming from inside.

Uncle George opens the door of the furnace and inside the children see all sorts of human beings in absolute agony: burning, screaming and shouting and Uncle George closes it very quickly and informs the children that if they don't behave, that is where they'll go.

The children are frightened into submission. When they come back up to meet their father and mother, Uncle George gives them lunch and then they drive home again.

On the way home the mother and father remind the children of how nice Uncle George was to them. And the children nod in agreement. 'And don't you love Uncle George with all your heart and all your soul?' mother asks. And even though they loathe the monster, the children say, 'Yes, I do', because anything else would mean they would have to join the queue for the furnace.

At that tender age a religious schizophrenia sets in. We keep telling Uncle George, how much we love him, and that we want to do only what pleases him and we dare not admit that we loathe him, because we are afraid of the consequences. And as soon as we grow away from Uncle George, we are delighted to get rid of him for once and for all out of our lives.

It is up to each of us today to question ourselves about our own image of God. I suspect God as Uncle George the tyrant will strike a chord with many of us. It's a question of whether we want to believe the infantile religion we were taught or to believe the word of God who once again reminds us that God so loved the world that he gave his only son so that we would be happy forever.

And God considers each of us to be a work of art.

That's the choice we have to make today. Before we stand to pray, 'I believe in one God,' perhaps we should take a few minutes to consider the image of this God we profess our belief in.

FOR MOTHER'S DAY

3 April 2011

I was going through some files and came across this lovely little piece which a daughter wrote about her mother. She began by saying her mother came to visit her and asked her to go shopping with her because she needed a new dress. The daughter admitted that she wasn't a patient person and didn't like shopping for herself never mind for other people. But because it was her mother they set off to the High Street together.

'We visited nearly every store that carried ladies dresses and my mother tried on dress after dress and rejected them all. As the day wore on, I grew irritable and my mother grew frustrated. Finally at our last stop my mother tried on a lovely dress which suited her. The blouse had a bow at the neckline, and as I stood in the dressing room with her I watched as she tried with much difficulty to tie the bow. Her hands were so badly crippled with arthritis that she couldn't do it.

'Suddenly as I watched her fumbling with arthritic hands it hit me. My impatience gave way to an overwhelming wave of compassion for this woman, my mother. I went over to tie the bow for her. The dress was beautiful and she bought it.

'Our shopping trip was over but the event etched itself indelibly in my mind. For the rest of the day my mind returned to that moment in the dressing room and to the vision of my mother's hands trying to tie that bow. They are old and stiff now but I couldn't get it out of my mind that these were the loving hands that fed me, bathed me, dressed me, tied my shoelaces and bows, caressed and comforted me and, most of all, prayed for me.

'Later that evening I went to my mother's room, took her hands in mine, kissed them, and, to me they were the most beautiful hands in the world …

'I can only pray, that my hands, will have earned such a beauty of their own.'

A full-time housewife had to go to a government department to apply for a licence. She was asked if she had a job and when she snapped that she was a mother, the girl in the office replied, 'We don't list "mother" as an occupation, "housewife" covers it.'

It too left an indelible imprint on the woman's self-confidence. So the next time in the same office when she was asked what her occupation was, she answered, 'I am a Research Associate in the field of Child Development and Human Relations.' The clerk wrote her rather pompous title into the official questionnaire. And when she had it written she asked, 'Might I just ask what you do in your field?' The woman replied, 'I have a continuing programme of research in the laboratory and in the field. I am working for my Masters (the whole family) and already have four credits (all daughters). Of course the job is one of the most demanding in humanities and I often work fourteen hours a day. But the job is more challenging than most run-of-the-mill careers and the rewards are in satisfaction rather than just money.'

The woman continued, 'There was an increasing note of respect in the clerk's voice. She completed the form and personally ushered me to the door. As I drove into my driveway buoyed by my glamorous new career, I was greeted by three of my lab assistants – aged thirteen, seven and three. And upstairs I could hear my next experimental model (six months old) in the child development programme testing out a new vocal pattern.

'I felt triumphant because in the official records I am now someone more distinguished and indispensable to society than anyone else. I am a mother.'

FATHER'S RULES

22 January 2012

Paul Flanagan was a young father who lost his battle with cancer, leaving two young heartbroken children behind. In his last weeks he wrote, 'A Father's Rules for Finding Fulfilment,' for his children. Here's part of what he wrote:

A Father's Rules for Finding Fulfilment

- Be courteous, be punctual, always say please and thank you, and be sure to hold your knife and fork properly. Others take their cue on how to treat you from your manners.

- Be kind, considerate and compassionate when others are in trouble, even if you have problems of your own. Others will admire your selflessness and will help you in due course.

- Show moral courage. Do what is right, even if that makes you unpopular. I always thought it important to be able to look at myself in the shaving mirror every morning and not feel guilt or remorse. I depart this world with a pretty clear conscience.

- Learn from your mistakes. If you keep making the same mistake ... you're doing something wrong.

* If someone crosses you, don't react immediately. Once you say something it can never be taken back, and most people deserve a second chance.

* Always respect age, as age equals wisdom.

* Be proud of who you are and where you come from, but open your mind to other cultures and languages. When you begin to travel (as I hope you will), you'll learn that your place in the world is both vital and insignificant. Don't get too big for your boots!

* Live every day to its fullest: do something that makes you smile or laugh, and avoid procrastination.

* Give of your best at school. Some teachers forget that pupils need incentives. So if your teacher doesn't give you one, devise your own.

* Look after your body and it will look after you.

* Learn a language, or at least try. Never engage a person abroad in conversation without first greeting them in their own language; by all means ask if they speak English!

* And finally, cherish your mother, and take very good care of her.'

Daddy Paul Flanagan

THAT'S FAMILY

A reader once asked me to write something to help her sort out her family problems. Let me put this gently – I can't sort your family out. For two reasons. Firstly it's over fifty years since I lived in a normal home. I have no experience of actually living in a modern family. Secondly, each family does it for themselves. What I can do is highlight a few areas to work on.

A family should be a safe place to be yourself. It's where you learn to love and to be loved. You should be able to make mistakes and still be accepted for who you are. You can grow, mature and pick up life's skills without pretence and without fear. That's a family's first function.

In a family secrecy is the enemy of good relationships. Parents are often more concerned about what the neighbours think than about the welfare of the precious little people in their care. Futures have been sacrificed to protect the good name of the family. That's wrong. Be open, be honest, and be forgiving. Don't judge harshly. Secrecy has allowed addicts to beat their spouses, children to be abused and bullies to get away with it.

Just accept that there is no such thing as a perfect family. Perfect families don't exist. Make the most out of what you've got. Enjoy the journey together and don't allow problems to dominate.

You can't solve every problem. There are some problems which are not meant to be solved. Embarrassingly, sometimes *you* are the problem.

Finally, the family that hugs together stays together. Great big passionate hugs are the best healers on earth. After you've hugged, talk and talk and talk until there's nothing left to say. Then eat your fill of hot and delicious food around the biggest, sturdiest table you can find. Forgiveness, fun, food – that's family.

A CRUST AROUND THE HEART

25 March 2012

A little breather in preparation for what the season of Lent is all about – the Passion, Death and Resurrection of Jesus. The readings ask us to contrast darkness and light (as the clocks move to the summertime) and challenges us to change and grow and die to the past, if we are to experience new life.

There is a very good film with the unusual title of *Extremely Loud and Incredibly Close* and it's a story of a boy's search for understanding and healing as a result of what happened to him on the infamous day of 9/11.

Oskar Shell is a bright but slightly dysfunctional eleven-year-old. He's close to his dad Thomas who tries to understand that his son is intelligent but lacks the ability to communicate with others. So he invents games to bring Oskar out of himself. Then Thomas is killed in the collapse of the World Trade Centre. Oskar is devastated and grows even more isolated from everyone and especially from his long-suffering mum.

When the funeral is over Oskar begins to search through some of his father's possessions. There he finds an envelope with the word, 'Black' written on it. Inside the envelope is a key. Oskar concludes that the key must be one more of his father's games. So he sets off on the rather difficult task of finding the lock which this key will open. Of course it is unrealistic and is indicative of the boy's dysfunction.

But Oskar's quest doesn't turn out the way he expects. He meets all kinds of people as he meticulously plans to find the lock which the key will open. In the process he has to talk about himself and his dad. He also has to listen to other people talking about themselves too. He learns simple things like the value of smiles, tears, hugs and prayers. Slowly as he matures he begins to understand he is not alone in his grief and that others – especially his mother Linda – have suffered loss as well.

He grows out of his fears; he also grows out of the behaviours which masked his fears, his rudeness, his obsessiveness, his impatience, his isolation from others. Almost despite himself he discovers that he is capable of loving and being loved. He also realises that he can cope with life even when it doesn't make sense. As the film points out, he was able to move beyond the worst days, to much better days.

A person without fear is not a hero. A person who overcomes fear is a hero.

Jean Vanier, the man who founded Faith and Light tells a lovely story about his companion, Jean Claude in L'Arche Community. Jean Claude suffers from Down's Syndrome. He's a happy individual and as Vanier said in the interview, 'He doesn't have a crust around his heart.'

One day Vanier was meeting a businessman. Jean Claude brought in the tea. He left down his tray and shook hands with Jean Vanier and said a very loud 'good morning' to him. He shook the hand of the businessman and gave him a big hug. The businessman couldn't cope with this, so as soon as Jean Claude had left the room he said, 'Isn't it sad to see a child like that?'

This annoyed Vanier. The businessman's own sadness had blocked out Jean Claude's joy. Jean Claude lives in his heart; The businessman lives in his head. The businessman truly had a crust around his heart.

And the businessman asked Jean Vanier what would happen to Jean Claude. Vanier answered, 'Perhaps if he is lucky he will fall sick and a hospital nurse will befriend him; maybe he will discover what is most important is his heart, so that he can love and be loved even if other things go wrong.'

The 'crust around the heart' is a great phrase. It certainly challenged me to see what sort of crust I put around mine to protect myself. Unless a grain of wheat dies … only when the crust is broken can the heart learn to love/live.

The bottom line today is that broken things are beautiful. As I have often said, it takes the broken soil to produce a new crop. It takes a broken cloud to produce new rain. It takes a broken grain of seed to make bread. It takes broken bread to give us friendship. It takes a broken person to be pieced together in God's image. And all this happened, as we will learn in the next few weeks, because the broken body of Christ was taken down from the cross, locked in a tomb, but burst out of the tomb to new life.

THE TAXI MAN

11 March 2012

It was George Burns, the great comedian who lived to be one hundred years old, who once said, 'The trouble with the world today is that those who know how to run it are, unfortunately, otherwise engaged cutting hair and driving taxis.'

It's true that some professions are at the cutting edge of life. Taxi drivers are one of them. Which is why this story from a taxi driver is so interesting. There are many versions of this story – this is how I tell it. I don't know the exact details but the truth in the story is too good to ignore.

One night he received a call to go to a small apartment in the city at 2.30 a.m. Thinking he was about to pick up some late night partygoers he was surprised to find a small woman in her eighties waiting to be collected. It seemed inappropriate that such a fragile and vulnerable lady should be travelling at so late an hour.

She wore a flowery dress and an old-fashioned pillbox hat. She had a small plastic bag by her side. He noticed that her flat was empty, except for a few pieces of furniture which she'd covered with sheets. There was a cardboard box floor filled with photos. The taxi man picked up her bag and helped her out to the car.

She gave him the address of her destination and then added, 'Could you take me through the city on the way, please?' He explained it was not the shortest way to where she was going. But she insisted. 'I don't mind,' she said. 'I am in no hurry. I am on my way to a hospice. I don't have to be there until the morning. I don't have any family left. The doctors say I don't have very long to live.'

She said it in a matter of fact sort of way and the driver knew she was serious. He switched off his meter and said he'd take her wherever she wanted to go.

For almost two hours they drove through the city. She pointed out the building where she used to work in her younger days; the house where she and her late husband lived when they were newly-wed; the furniture store which was once a ballroom was where she went dancing as a girl.

Sometimes she would ask him to slow down at particular buildings. She would sit staring into the darkness as her life replayed like a video in her mind.

The dawn was beginning to break when she finally said, 'I'm tired, we can go to the hospice now.'

Two attendants arrived with a wheelchair to help her out of the car. She asked the driver how much it cost. He refused to take a penny. 'You have to make a living,' she said.

'There are other passengers,' he replied.

'Well you gave an old woman a happy couple of hours,' she said as she was wheeled through the doors of the hospice.

The taxi man reflecting on his experience, later added, 'We often think our lives evolve around great moments. But in fact great moments often catch us unawares. There haven't been many days in my life when I thought, I was put on this earth to do just that. That experience with a frail old lady was one of those days. I know I have done nothing more important in my entire life.'

That's what keeps us going in these difficult times. That's what gives us hope. The most ordinary and mundane parts of our lives, the day-to-day activities, are where we find fulfillment.

FRIENDSHIP

Ever since I heard The Beatles singing 'I'll get by with a little help from my friends,' I realised how lucky I am to have good friends. Then it struck me how many different kinds of friends I have in my life.

Oscar Wilde wrote, 'Anyone can sympathise with the sufferings of a friend but it takes a very fine nature to sympathise with a friend's success.'

It takes a long time to cultivate a lasting friendship because it's when the going gets tough that you learn who your real friends are.

I like the theory which says we have three kinds of friends – those who come into our lives for a reason, those who come for a season and the few who last a lifetime.

Those who come for a reason usually meet some passing need in our lives. A relationship breaks down and an unexpected acquaintance befriends us as a shoulder to cry on. Yet as soon as we are able to cope on our own, they move on – they've done their job. They came for a reason; their friendship was real; it's just that we've both grown through it.

Those who come for a season enter our lives because of some special circumstance. When I lived in Africa for a short time, I made dozens of new friends who helped me settle in. I brought them a different vision of life and they showed me how to be happy in the midst of dreadful poverty. They were delightful friends for a season. I'll never forget them but I haven't seen them for twenty years and in all probability I'll never see them again.

A lasting friend however, knows you're a good egg even when you're cracked. A lifetime friend is God's way of taking care of us. Goethe said that when we treat people as if they were what they ought to be, we help them to become what they are capable of being.

But for me it was the poet and philosopher Camus who put it best of all when he wrote: 'Don't walk in front of me, I may not follow; don't walk behind me, I may not lead; walk beside me and be my friend.'

JOHN O'DONOHUE

28 August 2011

The writings of the Irish poet, philosopher and bestselling author, John O'Donohue, have helped thousands of seekers, including myself, to find God in the world of nature, beauty and love.

I had a few memorable conversations with John O'Donohue when both of us were priests in Ireland at a time when the role of the priest was changing, due mainly to the revelations about child sexual abuse among the clergy. John's writings were deep and philosophical. I tried to communicate to the masses through radio, television and the tabloids.

The first time I met John was at one of his lectures to a small, mixed group of priests and laity. The laity lapped up everything he said. The priests found it confusing. Afterwards we chatted about our different roles. Over coffee he told me of a contest, once held in Ancient Greece. The task was to write a sentence which would be eternally true. The sentence which won was 'This too shall pass.'

When I told him I was finding it difficult to stay in the priesthood he replied, 'Always remember that an horizon is something towards which we continually move but then discover that it moves with us.' It was his way of telling me that change is part of life.

Afterwards he sent me a note which I wish I had kept. I remember this part of it, 'We are infinitely greater than our minds; we are greater than our own images of ourselves.'

John believed that both fear and death are sisters which conspire to prevent us from living fully.

John O'Donohue died at the young age of fifty-two on 4 January 2008. He was born in 1956, the eldest of four children, to Patrick and Josie O'Donohue. They lived on a farm near the incredibly beautiful Burren area of Co. Clare. His father was a deeply religious man who found God in nature. John recalls hearing his father praying to God as he cared for the cows and sheep on the farm. The religious influence helped John, who was a bright student, to enter the seminary to study for the priesthood at Maynooth College when he was eighteen years old.

He was ordained in 1982 and subsequently learned German so that he could work on a doctorate at the University of Tübingen in Germany. He studied the philosophy of Hegel, of whom John wrote: 'He struck me as someone who put his eye to the earth at a most unusual angle and managed to glimpse the circle toward which all things aspire.'

In the early 1990s John combined his priestly duties with a post-doctorate study on the thirteenth-century philosopher and mystic Meister Eckhart. In 1997 he published the million-selling book *Anam Cara*. It succeeded in bringing Celtic spirituality to a new audience. 'Anam Cara' is an ancient Celtic phrase which literally means 'Soul Friend'. For John the ancient Celts never separated the visible from the invisible, time from eternity, or the human from the divine.

Eventually John resigned from priestly ministry to concentrate on writing and because he found it increasingly difficult to live a life of integrity within the hierarchical structures of the church. As he wrote in *Anam Cara*, 'The heart is the inner face of your life … love is absolutely vital for a human life. For love alone can awaken what is divine within you … When you learn to love and let yourself be loved, you come home to the heart of your own spirit. You are warm and sheltered.'

John's books are littered with beautiful poems, prayers and blessings. The last book he wrote is *Benedictus: A Book of Blessings*, published a few months before his death. Right at the end he includes a prayer for peace. This prayer highlights not only his desire for peace, but his ability to highlight the causes of war.

> We pray for all who suffered violence today
> May an unexpected serenity surprise them.
> For those who risk their lives each day for peace
> May their hearts glimpse providence at the heart of history.
> That those who make riches from violence and war
> Might hear in their dreams the cries of the lost.
> That we might see through our fear of each other
> A new vision to heal our fatal attraction to aggression.
> That those who enjoy the privilege of peace
> Might not forget their tormented brothers and sisters.

O'Donohue's father once told him, 'Life is like a mist on the hillside. It's there for a while, then it goes and you'll barely know if it was there at all.' In other words our time here is fleeting and for O'Donohue it was all too fleeting. After he resigned from the ministry he experienced the beauty of human love. He died suddenly, in France, whilst visiting the family of his partner.

He never regretted becoming a priest, in fact shortly before he died he wrote, 'The best decision I ever made was to become a priest, and I think the second best decision was to resign from public priestly ministry.' He found the system more a burden than a gift.

Throughout his writings the influence of Meister Eckhart is obvious. Eckhart believed that the divine is that which is totally and utterly itself. We can touch the divine but never exhaust it. O'Donohue recalled, 'Meister Eckhart says that the soul has two faces. One faces towards the world, and the other faces towards the divine, where it receives "the kiss of God" … there is a place in the soul that neither time, nor flesh, nor no creative thing can touch.' Later O'Donohue wrote: 'The divine is like a huge smile that breaks somewhere in the sea within you, and gradually comes up again. It's an incredible, intimate thing. It's every bit as intimate as sexuality, and as human love.'

Let me sum up much of what John O'Donohue believes with a quote from *Benedictus: A Book of Blessings*:

> *As the wind loves to call things to dance*
> *May your gravity be lightened by grace …*
>
> *May your prayer of listening deepen enough*
> *To hear, in the depths, the laughter of God.*

STORYTELLING

6 May 2012

I was in Kerry on Friday at a wedding. The beautiful hotel in Killarney looked out over the lakes with the mountains of Kerry sitting on top of the lakes. It was a panoramic view of God's nature at its best, a view which changed every ten minutes. The Celtic people loved nature and found God in everything – you could see why in Killarney. They had a respectful fear of the God of the sea, the mountains, the wind, earth and sky. They didn't see different gods. They saw the mighty God living and breathing within them as a source of all their gifts and they were careful to be grateful.

There's an old Celtic story of Goban and his only son. Before he died he wanted to get to know his son so he decided to go on a journey with him. On the first day Goban said to his son, 'Please help me to shorten the journey.' Goban's son took it literally and cut corners, took shortcuts across fields and tried to shorten the journey physically. That was not what Goban wanted so he decided to return home. Next day they started out with greater hope. Once again on the journey Goban said to his son, 'Help me to shorten the journey.' And this time the son asked the father to explain in detail the castle he would build when he would reach the end of his journey together. This is not what Goban wanted so they returned home again. The son was distracted now and asked his mother to help him to do what was right for his father. And the mother did help him. On the third day Goban and his son started off again and when Goban said, 'Son help me to shorten the journey,' the son began to tell him his story, his life, his dreams, his difficulties. And before they knew it they were at their destination.

Stories are important in our lives. Our own stories particularly. Each of us has a story, but each of us is helped by everyone else's story too. Everyone's story gives meaning to life; it helps imagination, it inspires memories, it brings vision, it's full of metaphor. In short every story is partly my story too.

Jesus told stories that challenged and changed and disturbed people. His stories also taught people unforgettable lessons for life.

Don't be afraid to take time and reflect on your story. John Lennon was correct when he philosophised, 'Life is what happens whilst we are making other plans.'

Brendan Behan was a genius who concluded, 'Talent borrows, but genius steals.' I am not genius enough to steal someone's idea and make it my own but I am cute enough to borrow the ideas of others when it is best to do so. The poet Robert Frost is the one I am borrowing from today:

> *Were epitaph to be my story*
> *I'd have a short one ready for my own.*
> *I'd have written of me on my stone*
> *I had a lovers quarrel with the world.*

In a sense that's the story of each of our lives. We have an ongoing love-hate relationship with ourselves, with the world, with the church, with everything. But it's a lover's quarrel not a harmful one. We always know that, 'no one is so rich that they can be without friends.' The gospel mentioned vine branches. Jesus was a country man who understood his audience and his audience understood vines and how vines are a symbol of a community. They grow together and one little grape won't make much wine but a whole vineyard of grapes will. It takes every single one to do it but all of them have to work as a community too.

The second reading today (John 3:18–24) makes an important point: There are some helpful quotes in it. 'Our love is not just to be mere talk but something real and active … My dear people if we cannot be condemned by our conscience we need not be afraid in God's presence.' What a wonderful insight that is.

And lastly his commandments are these. That we believe in the name of his Son Jesus Christ; that we love one another as he told us. Belief in Jesus and love – make those the basis of our lives and we will never go too far wrong.

Cardinal Newman said, 'A thousand difficulties do not amount to one doubt.' We should accept ourselves as we are and not expect for the impossible. Newman also said, 'The perfect is the enemy of the good.' So many are being put off by people wanting to be perfect when God is happy with us just trying our best.

Maybe it is all best summed up today in this little piece:

God won't ask you what kind of car you drove,
   But he will ask you how many people you drove who didn't have
   a car.
God won't ask you the size of your house,
   But he will ask you how many people you welcomed into your
   home.
God won't ask you how much overtime you worked,
   But he will ask how much overtime really benefited your family.
God won't ask you how many promotions you received in your life,
   But he will ask you how much encouragement you gave to
   others.
God won't ask you how many friends you had in your life,
   But he will ask you how much of a friend you are to other people.
God won't ask you in what neighbourhood you live in,
   But he will ask you how you treated your neighbours no matter
   where you lived.

THE SIGNS OF INNER PEACE

20 November 2011

We need to be on the lookout for symptoms of inner peace … It is possible that people everywhere could collapse with it in epidemic proportions.

This could pose a serious threat to the condition known as conflict in the world. Here are some signs and symptoms of inner peace which should alarm you:

- A tendency to think and act spontaneously rather than on fears based on past experience.

- An unmistakable ability to enjoy each moment.

- Loss of interest in being judgemental of other people.

- Loss of interest in conflict of all kinds.

- Loss of ability to worry – in itself a serious symptom of inner peace.

- Frequent overwhelming episodes of appreciation.

- Contented feelings of connectedness with others and with nature.

- Frequent attacks of smiling and even laughter.

- An increased tendency to let things happen rather than the urge to make them happen.

If you have two or more of these symptoms, you are in grave danger of being out of step with the rest of the world.

REAL CATHOLICS OR
Á LA CARTE CATHOLICS

22 April 2012

There was consensus on at least one point when the Association of Catholic Priests published the survey they commissioned on the religious views held by practicing Catholics in Ireland – the findings merely confirmed what most people already knew.

If there was a surprise, it was that 35% of Catholics on the island of Ireland still attend Mass at least once a week and 50% once a month – surely one of the highest percentages in Europe.

The survey showed that 87% believe priests should be allowed to marry; 77% believe women should be ordained; 72% that married men should be accepted for ordination. Another 87% support allowing divorced/separated Catholics, now in second relationships, to receive Communion.

Anyone with an ear to the ground appreciates that these figures accurately reflect what practicing Catholics in Ireland believe could happen. These views have become acceptable to many over the last fifteen to twenty years. The majority of the people who have thought about their religion have come to these conclusions as a result of their lived experience. They see themselves as neither lapsed nor liberal.

It is not the result of predatory priests abusing innocent children nor is it a result of the cover-ups which followed. Rather life itself has enabled many committed Catholics to have an adult relationship with God.

The figures would, of course, be different if the large number of former believers, who now view Catholicism with apathy or, worse still, hostility, were taken into account.

Facts are not our problem but rather what should we do now.

Some, though not many, argue that the Catholic Church should change its rules because the people have spoken. But even a moment's reflection would convince us that our church's beliefs cannot be based on surveys and polls. It is, however, vital that we deal with the facts and don't ignore them. This survey should help us to focus our dialogue.

Others are convinced that à la carte Catholics are the real problem. They argue that because so many believers favour changes to the structures and regulations, the church must instead stick to its guns and dump these misguided 'dissidents' out of the Catholic Church altogether. Rome should then fight a rearguard action using the might of the 'Real Catholics'.

For these 'Real Catholics' the church is a club with its own rules and regulations. If you don't like the rules, get out of the club. Priests like me, for example, should have 'the party whip withdrawn from them' as one prominent Catholic woman so smugly put it on a radio programme recently.

But we know that our beautiful church is not a club or a political party or a horrible multinational with a head office in Rome. Our church is the life of the Trinity on earth. Through the Passion, Death and Resurrection of Jesus; our community grows, loves, forgives, and generously offers compassion to the weak and the struggling.

Our church, Christ showed us, can never be limited by human small-mindedness but instead reaches out to the marginalised with the Good News of salvation. Our church is always in need of renewal and is always willing to be renewed. Christ's true church cherishes the people of God and thrives on respectful dialogue. It is neither a democracy nor a dictatorship. Our church is above all a listening church because we believe the Holy Spirit is alive in all its members.

Sadly in our church now, it has become impossible to be open and honest about what good people are convinced of. It's as if merely stating unpalatable facts is in itself disloyal. For years I've tried to point out the perils of the growing disconnect between church leaders and the ordinary people which in fact has forced believers to discern their own path to God.

It's not as if the Association's survey figures apply only to the Irish church; surveys of believers in many countries in the developed world have come up with very similar results. Thankfully we now know what the majority of Catholics in Ireland privately believe. Whether or not we agree with the survey's figures it would be sinful not to welcome the genuine dialogue being offered to us.

As mature believers we should use this graced opportunity to renew our church and to take heart from the experiences of genuine believers searching for truth in this changing world.

CIARÁN ENRIGHT

19 June 2011

As far as I know I have never met, nor have I spoken to, Fr Ciarán Enright, the full-time prison chaplain who was mentioned in *The Sunday World* as being a 'close pal' of Larry Murphy. Murphy spent over ten years in prison after he was convicted of serious and reprehensible crimes. He was released in controversial circumstances, last year. Fr Enright was one of those who continually tried, unsuccessfully, to convince Murphy to enter a meaningful counselling programme.

The article was critical of Fr Enright for helping Murphy, inside and outside the prison, and for highlighting the manner in which Murphy was treated by the State and by the press, after his release from prison on completion of his sentence. Fr Enright was described as 'the only friend in the world' and 'a sidekick' of Larry Murphy.

When I read it first I was annoyed because I thought it was unfair to Fr Enright. So I left it aside until I cooled down. When I read it again, some days later, I knew I had to say something about this issue because, to my mind, it goes to the heart of what a priest is supposed to be.

As a prison chaplain it was Ciarán Enright's duty to do what he could to ensure that Murphy was treated in a proper way. There are laws about how prisoners, no matter how heinous their crime, must be treated. More to the point, the gospels make it clear that the marginalised and the rejected – which prisoners are – must be treated with respect and should be given every opportunity to reform their lives. That's not a popular principle in today's society, but it is what gospel witness demands, whatever the consequences.

Had Fr Enright deserted the prisoner, he would not have done his duty. This is not me defending another member of the clerical club. It's me stating a conviction about the true nature of priesthood. A priest's calling is to be brave, vocal, and compassionate. If a priest does not devote himself fearlessly to making God's love accessible to everyone, then he is not a priest.

Just in case there is any doubt about it, I abhor what Murphy did. I also realise from those who should know, that he appears to be quite capable of doing terrible deeds again unless he undergoes a complete change of behaviour. Society needs to be protected from unrepentant criminals. Furthermore, I hope, and presume, that other priests/ministers are caring for the families of his victim – if they require it.

The point I'm making here, though, is that it is unfair and unjustifiable to condemn a prison chaplain for caring for a prisoner. That's his vocation. It's what a prison chaplain does. The State decides who should go to prison; chaplains should care for all of those sent there.

I believe that as a priest I should devote my life to helping people most in need of help. I have spent a good portion of my life helping prisoners and other rejects of society. My great regret, and it gets more disturbing as I get older, is that I didn't do enough for the downtrodden. I wasted most of my life doing 'churchy' duties and not nearly enough doing what Fr Enright does.

I believe a priest should be willing to give 'nothing less than everything' to defend the little people from the hypocrisy of societies and institutions (including churches). I would rather live out the rest of my short life outside the priesthood than agree to remain silent about grave injustices.

In the 1980s and 1990s I was asked to mediate in four kidnapping incidents. I was reminded by the Gardaí that I could be killed as a result. I believed then and I believe now, that it would be better for an unattached, single man like me to lose my life than it would be for a father or someone with a future, to lose theirs. Again, I believe it's what a priest is for.

As I've said, I don't know Ciarán Enright but I agree whole-heartedly with him when he's quoted as saying: 'Irish prisons have become more like warehouses for the poor and vulnerable, offering little or no hope to many of those imprisoned … the current prison system is dysfunctional and in need of radical change.' Later in the Whittaker Committee Report *20 Years On* he concludes: 'As a person of hope, I believe that change is always possible, that it is never too late to learn' (p. 101).

That's it in a nutshell – hope and the possibility of redemption. I believe it is a priest's duty to keep on hoping, especially when society and even his church disown him. A priest should resist injustice everywhere but especially institutionalised injustice; he should stand up for the weak and voiceless; help the suffering; withstand the attempts of the powerful to silence the voice of the prophet; he should be a person of integrity and he should promote justice, truth and love above all else.

Archbishop Helder Camara summed it up perfectly when he said: 'When I feed the hungry, they call me a saint; but when I ask why the poor are hungry, they call me a Communist.'

My bottom line is: Don't belittle Ciarán Enright – support him!

Outcasts

12 February 2012

Are we on the inside looking out at the outcasts or are we outcasts looking in at a club that we can never hope to be part of?

Here's a story that does have a point if you'll bear with me. One day Moses, Jesus and another old man with a beard went out to play golf. They were doing very well and Moses was asked to tee off. He meticulously placed the ball, concentrated on his swing, got the proper driver and sent it straight into the middle of the water hazard lake. He cursed and then thought for a moment. He charged down to the lake, parted the water, as Moses always does, walked in and took the ball out of the pond.

Jesus was very impressed as he was next to go. He put the ball down and was equally careful about his stance, but he hooked his swing and once again it went straight into the water hazard lake. Well Jesus didn't curse, he simply went down to the lake walked across it, saw where the ball was, picked it up and played on.

At this stage they were beginning to feel very sorry for the old man who had to compete with them. He put the ball down and took a little time before driving the ball. It seemed to be a wonderful shot but at the last minute, it too faded into the lake. The old man went down to the lake, peered into the water with a look of desolation and then was delighted to see a fish come swimming along. However, he wasn't delighted when the fish swallowed his golf ball. The fish swam up to the top of the lake and as he did a hawk came, swooped down, lifted the fish and carried it off. The poor old man was left with nothing. But then as the hawk was flying with the fish and the ball inside the fish, a flash of lightening struck the bird. The bird and the fish disintegrated but the ball dropped down onto the green two inches from the hole and rolled straight in.

Jesus looked at the old man with the beard and said, 'Great shot Dad!'

The moral of the story is you never know where God is. And just when we think all the religious leaders had got the better of him, God can step in for a hole in one.

When it comes to talking about lepers the first reading is vitally important. There we see what the Book of Leviticus outlined for these poor people. The person was unclean, he had to go to the priest to be declared unclean. He was forced to wear torn clothing lest he be taken for a respectable person. His hair must be dishevelled and he must go around ringing a bell crying, 'unclean, unclean'. And then it ends with, 'He must live outside the camp.' Can you imagine a more desolate life for anyone than being forced to live with leprosy?

And yet Jesus knowing what the penalty was for speaking to a leper must have shown his compassion at sometime because the gospel begins by saying that a leper came to Jesus and 'pleaded on his knees'. The leper was not afraid of Jesus. He was confident that Jesus would cure him. In fact he tells him, 'If you want to you can cure me.'

Jesus must have shown compassion to others in similar situations. He always made the outsider part of the family. The leper was confident he would do it again. Jesus had a threefold ministry.

1. *He stretched out his hand.* That's wonderful to remember that Jesus, when we are feeling down or depressed, always stretches his hand. The hand of welcome, the hand of courage. He gives us a hand to get up.

2. *He touched him.* Obviously he touched him physically which meant that Jesus now had to suffer the same indignity as a leper, he became one of the lepers as soon as he touched him. He also touched him in the wider sense in that he touched him deep in his soul.

3. *He healed him.* Jesus is making it quite clear how we are to deal with the outcasts; this is how we are to make outcasts feel welcome in God's kingdom. The leper in his despair turned to Jesus and Jesus did not disappoint him.

One of the messages of the gospel today is that labels which exclude people are obnoxious. There are many labels: Unmarried mother, poor person, gay person, unemployed person and many more highlighting colour and status. They are all obnoxious labels for people with small minds. When we can't cope with difference we label it and dismiss it. But Christians should not do that. Christians should welcome the outcasts.

As an example of this I remember doing an interview with Cliff Richard many years ago. Like all born-again Christians he was articulate in describing his life before he became a Christian. It was a life according to him of sex, drugs and rock n' roll. You can hardly imagine Sir Cliff being like that now. But then who wasn't like that as a teenager. However when he became a pop star he met Billy Graham and through his influence Cliff turned his life around and became a born-again Christian. Cliff said for many years after that he felt superior to others. It's the 'once I was lost but now I am found' mentality. He was special in his own eyes.

Later, to his credit, he realised that Christianity is more than feeling smug. So he decided to help children through the Tear Fund. He went out to Bangladesh on a publicity shoot early on. But when he got there he discovered he wasn't able to face the children. He thought they were too dirty, too sick, too awful to be in contact with. Yet he had to get publicity pictures for the Tear Fund. He went down on his knee beside one of the children, and as the photographer tried to get the best shot, he stood on the fingers of the little child, who roared out in pain.

Without even thinking Cliff lifted the little child, hugged it and calmed it down before realising what he had done. He believes that really was the moment of his conversion. He recognised that a helpless, vulnerable poor little child was more important than his squeamishness.

They say that those in trouble can always ring the Samaritans. But if the Samaritans ring you, you are in real trouble. I must be a tough case. Because the Samaritans rang me during the week. They were looking for publicity. They wanted me to talk about the twenty-four hour service they give to those in distress. They have helped five million such people each year in these small islands. The Samaritans treat the outcasts, the depressed, those whom nobody else wants anything to do with. Those who are about to take their own life. The Samaritans listen to them, they heal. That is practical Christianity.

St Paul in the second reading sums everything up perfectly with two phrases. In 1 Cor 10, 31, he writes, 'Never do anything offensive to anyone … try to be helpful to everyone at all times.' That's Christianity in a nutshell. Never harm another and try to help everyone.

One last point. At the beginning of the gospel we find Jesus was the hero, the accepted one, the one everyone wanted to be with. The leper was the outcast. He was the one nobody wanted to be with. By the end of the gospel, through the good influence of Jesus, it is the leper who is accepted in his community with joy and happiness. And it is Jesus who, 'had nowhere to go'. The leper was with the community and Jesus was struggling on his own. Somewhere in the middle of that paradox is what ministry is all about.

Signs of Hope

20 May 2012

I was asked to give a talk to a group of younger believers and at the end one of the young people in the church asked me, 'Well, Brian, do you see any sign of hope in the church?' They were talking about the Roman Catholic Church and I said, 'I do' and they said, 'what is it?' I replied, 'the collapse of clericalism'. That is the greatest sign of hope there can be because God is asking us, calling us, to build from the roots up, a new way of being Christian with one another.

Solzhenitsyn, the Russian novelist and historian, said that the culture of the West is in spiritual exhaustion. And yet the Book of Proverbs says that unless we have a vision the people will perish. Our job is to recognise our exhaustion and to look for the vision. My conviction is: you cannot think yourself into a new way of living. Christian communities live themselves into a new way of thinking.

The problem is that we won't allow ourselves to be different enough to live again. We keep thinking 'old,' imposing 'old,' when we know that God is calling us to be ever new: That is the challenge.

The basic question is: how can we allow ourselves to live differently enough so that we can live ourselves into a new way of thinking?

Ralph Waldo Emerson used to say that 'nothing great is ever achieved without enthusiasm' and that's a wonderful theological statement, actually, because 'enthusiasm' comes from the Greek words *en theos*, that is 'filled with God'. And that is what we are asked to do; to have an enthusiasm – to be filled with God.

In my reading of scripture I find very few examples where Jesus actually confronted the political and religious systems. Instead he simply taught us a new system. He gave us the Beatitudes as a model for a new way of living. He didn't break the old system, he simply ignored it. In ignoring it he founded a new way which people chose of their own free will as being new, different, compassionate and meaningful. We are at that point in Ireland. We need to be enthused, filled with God, led by God's spirit, so that like Jesus we can reform from the outside what appears irredeemable from the inside.

My hope is based on the conviction that God is good, that the world is good and that I am good. God created all things good. Jesus had a bias towards the bottom. Our old friend Archbishop Desmond Tutu put it magnificently, 'Jesus is always on the side of those being clobbered.' That's my theology, in a nutshell – Jesus is always on the side of those being clobbered.

Change is external, transition is internal. We are in transition. Anyone can change but very few choose to be in transition. Transition is a slow growth into darkness and homelessness and discovering that all the securities aren't there and then being shocked to find in the midst of the desolation of the desert of loneliness, that God is there. It's recognising the powerlessness exemplified by Jesus on the cross. When Jesus could move neither hand nor foot, salvation was accomplished. We have to learn to be content not to know. To be able to travel in trust. To know that our God is a God of love and to recognise that God is the only criterion of success. I must put my life in God's hands, 'Into your hands, I commend my spirit.' It is a safe place to be.

Let me finish with a prayer from one of my heroes in life. Thomas Merton went from atheism to some form of Christianity, to an unusual form of Roman Catholicism and eventually into a Trappist monastery. And in the Trappist monastery, where he was not allowed to speak, his writings became one of the major influences on the last century.

From his monastery Merton was able to not only be the architect of civil rights for Martin Luther King, Joan Baez, Bob Dylan and Bobby Kennedy but he was also able to be the one who united East and West in contemplation.

God works in the broken pieces, and this was Merton's prayer. I can honestly tell you that it is my prayer each night.

My Lord God, I have no idea where I am going.
I do not see the road ahead of me.
I cannot know for certain where it will end.
Nor do I really know myself,
and the fact that I think I am following your will
does not mean that I am actually doing so.
But I believe that the desire to please you
does in fact please you.
And I hope I have that desire in all that I am doing.
I hope that I will never do anything apart from that desire.
And I know that if I do this
you will lead me by the right road,
though I may know nothing about it.
Therefore I will trust you always
though I may seem to be lost in the shadow of death.
I will not fear, for you are with me,
and you will never leave me to face my perils alone.

Amen.

DESMOND TUTU

2 October 2011

Desmond Tutu was born on 7 October 1931 in a small gold-mining town in the Transvaal. He thought of following his father into teaching, but abandoned that career after the passage of the 1953 Bantu Education Act which enforced separation of races in all educational institutions.

He joined the Anglican clergy and was influenced by many white clergymen including Bishop Trevor Huddleston. In 1975 Desmond Tutu became the first black Anglican Dean of Johannesburg. He became Archbishop of Cape Town in 1986. Soon after he announced, 'We refuse to be treated as the doormat for the government to wipe its jackboots on.' Six months later, he risked jail by calling for a boycott of the municipal elections. In a short time he was able to welcome liberalising reforms announced by President F. W. de Klerk in 1989.

Following Nelson Mandela's release from prison in 1990, one of the greatest days of Archbishop Tutu's life was the free elections of 1994 in South Africa when Mandela was elected president. It was shortly after that President Mandela asked Archbishop Tutu to set up a Truth and Reconciliation Commission. It gathered evidence of the apartheid-era crimes and recommended whether people confessing their involvement should receive amnesty. It was a most trying and emotional part of Archbishop Tutu's life and he was often appalled at the evil uncovered. He retired from public life in 2010.

The wisdom of Desmond Tutu.

✸ Children are a wonderful gift. They have an extraordinary capacity to see into the heart of things and to expose sham and humbug for what they are.

✸ I don't preach a social gospel; I preach the gospel, period. The gospel of our Lord Jesus Christ is concerned for the whole person. When people were hungry, Jesus didn't say, 'Now is that political or social?' He said, 'I feed you.' Because the good news to a hungry person is bread.

✸ Our Lord would say that in the end the positive thing that can come is the spirit of forgiving. Not forgetting, but the spirit of saying, 'God, this happened to us. We pray for those who made it happen, help us to forgive them and help us so that we in our turn will not make others suffer.'

✸ We may be surprised at the people we find in heaven. God has a soft spot for sinners. His standards are quite low.

✸ God has such a deep reverence for our freedom that he'd rather let us freely go to hell than be compelled to go to heaven.

✸ Sometimes you want to whisper in God's ear, 'God, we know you are in charge, but why don't you make it slightly more obvious?'

✸ Freedom and liberty lose out by default because good people are not vigilant.

✸ Do your little bit of good where you are; it's those little bits of good put together that overwhelm the world.

✸ Resentment and anger are bad for your blood pressure and your digestion.

AFFLICT THE COMFORTABLE, COMFORT THE AFFLICTED

15 July 2012

St Swithin's Day. If it rains today it rains for forty days and forty nights. I think we should start petitioning Rome to change St Swithin's Day from 15 July to 12 July. That's the only way we are going to get it to work.

All of the readings today are trying to make the same points in different ways. To be a prophet, to be a Christian, means that we have to be dedicated, focused and fearless. We have to speak the truth in season and out of season and we have to live dedicated lives without allowing material things to take over our lives.

I was speaking recently to Alice Leahy whom I've known for nearly forty years. She helps the homeless and was one of the people who was asked to speak on behalf of the homeless at the Eucharistic Congress in Dublin.

In 1975 she and a number of other dedicated people, many of whom were doctors, founded an organisation called Trust. It was to help the homeless find a place of refuge, a place where they could be washed, checked medically, have some rest and be treated as human beings. It is situated halfway between St Patrick's Cathedral and Christ Church Cathedral in the centre of Dublin. We were renewing acquaintances about her work with the poor and she told me about one of her clients, Joe by name, who usually was a quiet grateful man, but who in recent days was suffering from a very serious depression. She tried to talk to him, to find out the reason for his unhappiness. Eventually he told her about an incident that happened a week beforehand. It was his practice to go into a Catholic Church, usually the Pro-Cathedral, each day. He might have gone in to find warmth, or just rest or maybe sleep in comfort, but he always attended Mass each day. He was sitting at the back of the Cathedral when the 'sign of peace' was called for by the priest. A woman two seats in front of him turned around to shake hands with him and when he put his hand out and she saw that he was old and dirty and smelly, she pulled her hand back and refused the 'sign of peace'. Joe said she went to Communion that day but he didn't feel worthy to do so. It had a devastating effect on him and it probably was 'the straw that broke the camel's back' for him. His hand was dirty and nicotine-stained. But had Joe not a very good point to make? We seem to be extraordinarily careful of ourselves. I could understand the woman. And yet the readings say today that the true disciple and the true prophet are called to be homeless and focused.

God seems to frequently call the powerless to preach to those imprisoned by power. Amos is a case in point. He is one of my Old Testament heroes. Amos was a small farmer who came from a tiny village in the hill country. He lived about 800 years before the time of Christ and his only training was in farming.

Amos had a call from God and the small farmer, with no training, became the prophet. He was so convinced of what he was doing that he left his small farm and his tiny village. Like many a small farmer before him, Amos was a simple man but he wasn't stupid. In fact he was the first prophet to commit his work to writing and he was a brilliant communicator, a gift which always seems to get prophets into more trouble than they expected. People understood what Amos was saying and clarity is dangerous. All around him was the equivalent of the Celtic Tiger. Israel then was at the highest point of its prosperity. The land was productive, the cities were eloquently built and the rich had their winter and summer villas.

However Amos knew that there was widespread corruption. The poor were exploited and sold into slavery. There was a show about religion but no justice. Amos didn't like it one bit. He said, 'I hate and despise your feasts … let me have no more of the den of your chanting … let justice flow like water and integrity, like an unfailing stream' (Amos 5:21–24).

The priests accused him of being disloyal. It's an old trick to attack the prophet who opposes the status quo. But it didn't work with Amos; he told them that loyalty to the word of God has priority over every other loyalty in life. The small farmer, the ordinary lay man with no training, was effective because he got his priorities right. He put God's word ahead of the institution.

The readings point out what a good disciple should do. God gives us every spiritual blessing. We are to be focused, taking no money, no clothes, no food, accepting what our hosts give us. We are to do something. Once we have spoken about God's integrity, then it's up to the people to accept it or reject it. Don't fight with them, but rather shake the dust of the place off your feet and move to spread God's word in another place. Sad will be the judgement of those who refuse to listen.

A Final Prayer

> Lord Disturb me when I am too well pleased with myself;
> When my dreams have come true because I dreamed too little;
> When I have sailed too close to the shore,
> Stir me up Lord to dare more boldly;
> To venture more seas where storms still show your mastery.
> And in losing sight of land I shall find the stars.

We must be brave, focused and listen to God's call. Be like Amos – afflict the comfortable and comfort the afflicted.

The Smaller Beatitudes

September 2011

Blessed are you who can laugh at yourselves: you will have no end of fun.

Blessed are you who can tell a mountain from a molehill: you will be saved a lot of bother.

Blessed are you who know how to relax without looking for excuses: you are on the way to becoming wise.

Blessed are you who know when to be quiet and listen: you will learn a lot of new things.

Blessed are you who are sane enough not to take yourselves too seriously: you will be valued by those around you.

Blessed are you if you can take small things seriously and face serious things calmly: you will go far in life.

Blessed are you if you can appreciate a smile and forget a frown: you will walk on the sunny side of the street.

Blessed are you who think before acting and pray before thinking: you will avoid many blunders.

Above all: Blessed are you who recognise the Lord in all whom you meet: the light of truth shines in your life for you have found true wisdom.

Author Unknown

Franz Liszt

17 April 2011

The famous pianist Franz Liszt was regarded as a musical genius in his time. For example, he pioneered the use of music in therapy.

He was once invited by Nicholas the First of Russia to perform at court. In the middle of the first sonata Liszt noticed that the Czar was talking to his aide. At first, the composer concealed his irritation and continued playing. But when the conversation became clearly audible Liszt stopped playing, bowed his head and rested his hands on his knees in silence.

Immediately the Czar sent his aide to find out why he stopped.

'When the Czar speaks,' Liszt replied, 'everyone should listen.' There were no more interruptions. How we handle anger and stress is important.

Anger is only one letter away from danger. Liszt clearly believed in the maxim: Don't get angry, get even.

Catholic Leadership

14 August 2011

I've always tried to be honest – I have no intention of leaving the priesthood, but yes I am finding it difficult. I don't know who to trust in the leadership of the Catholic Church.

Here's how I see it. For over two decades now the only story we are hearing, is about abusive priests and religious. There are glimpses of good news such as World Youth Day, a genuinely wonderful story of faith and hope. The problem is the main news stories about our church are bad news stories and rightly so. As bad as the abusive priests were, people find it more difficult to understand negligent diocesan officials all over the world, who put the protection of their institution, ahead of the protection of innocent children. Furthermore revelations about church criminality and sin, have not come voluntarily from the church itself. By and large it has come from:

1) The brave survivors and
2) diligent journalists doing what they are supposed to do.

We also have proof from independent reports, exposing the 'less than satisfactory' reaction of church officials to the most horrible crime and sin imaginable – the abuse of little children.

We have heard church officials reacting in shock to revelations that we now know they were aware of for decades. That more than anything, has destroyed the credibility of church leadership. It is the church leaders themselves who have fractured trust.

It's not fair to blame survivors, journalists and others who speak the truth. The blame for the sorry state of our church today lies directly at the hands of the leadership, as well as the obviously too docile clerical foot soldiers, who by our silence are part of the problem.

Worldwide, Enda Kenny's accusations against the Vatican have been welcomed as both timely, accurate and appropriate. Once again, whatever the truth of the matter is, the Vatican State's reaction has been seen as petty and lacking humility.

The morale of both the laity and the clergy has been undermined. The moral authority of the church has been tainted by cover-ups.

There is a sneaking feeling that the clerical church is still trying to hide something. Efforts to get at the truth are frustrated; statements of repentance are grudging; every layer of truth exposed, points unerringly to a system that has shielded abusers.

To be fair there is some good news. The hierarchy in Germany has made one prophetic step to reverse the trend. In July they voted unanimously to grant independent investigators full access to their files on sexual abuse by clergy going back to 1945. Unquestionably the findings will be shocking both in the extent of the abuse and the systemic failures in handling the allegations. So deep-rooted is the lack of trust in church leadership that even this offer is questioned. Investigators wonder if they will see the unaltered files.

To date the abuse crisis has hit North America and Western Europe most severely. Fewer allegations have come from Central and South America, India, Asia and indeed Africa. There are huge Catholic populations in these areas, all controlled by the Roman hierarchical model. It would be foolish to presume that there were no abusers in those cultures. My fear is that we face more decades of worldwide revelations as the crisis unravels.

The German bishops have admitted that they cannot reform and repent on their own. They have asked for help honestly and humbly. They recognise that once trust has been broken, it's impossible to put it together again.

The chasm between the clerical church and the believing laity is now immense. The laity knows that they acted properly in the essential matters of morality. Many clerics have to learn to be less arrogant, less dictatorial, more humble, more open and more willing to learn. Our only hope is that the seeds of genuine humility have been sown in many dioceses and religious congregations and that the promise of Jesus to be with us to the end of time takes effect.

FEAR

18 September 2011

An often-quoted extract from the inaugural speech of Nelson Mandela as President of South Africa is this brilliant piece of advice: 'Our deepest fear is not that we are inadequate. Our deepest fear is that we are powerful beyond measure.'

The words were actually written by Marianne Williamson and she has hit upon a great truth – too much of life is choked by irrational fears. We like to play small, because we are afraid of failure.

So what is it that we are afraid of? I have seen various acronyms for fear which attempt to answer the question. F-E-A-R. Does it mean, 'False Evidence Appearing Real' or does it mean 'Face Everything And Recover.' The choice is yours.

At different times in life a different fear grips us. It can even be an unconscious fear at first. Perhaps it is really a fear of the unconscious. It will show itself as a fear of disappointing our parents; fear of being in the public eye; for many it's the fear of being the centre of attention; for others it's the fear of not being the centre of attention.

When I take time to reflect on my life it is humbling to note how much fear dominates my decisions. Fear of failure, fear of success, fear of losing friendships; fear of making others feel inadequate; fear of rejection, fear of commitment.

At this point in my life I am simply reluctant to complicate my life any further. Why do I have to take any more risks? Why ruffle feathers when I don't need to? The temptation is to play small and stay as I am.

For somebody taking life seriously, playing safe and staying small is not an option. Life is about growth, maturity, honesty and integrity. We simply have to face some fear, real or imagined, and claim our deepest, truest selves. A plant cannot push itself back into a seed; it grows in the direction of the sun and light. We too gravitate towards enlightenment otherwise we die in darkness. The first step is to overcome our fear of change.

Seamus Heaney humorously analysed his parents. He said his mother's motto was, 'Whatever you say, say nothing.' She never put it into practice herself because she talked non-stop. His father, he said, was different. He could communicate but not with words. Heaney explains, 'Language was a kind of betrayal,' for his father. Those are two sides of every man and every woman.

Life is a journey of forgiveness but it is also a journey of self-awareness. T. S. Elliott summed up his own journey when he said:

> The end of all exploring
> will be to arrive where we started
> and know the place for the first time.

Ultimately it is an act of faith that God loves this struggling mixture of success and failure that I have become.

Sadly many of our churches insist that we be preachers of fear and obedience. Jesus, on the other hand, said that our lives should be based on love and compassion.

It has been said that the words, 'Do not be afraid,' or 'Do not fear,' are used in the Bible 365 times. I have never checked that out but I have been assured that it is correct. It seems that God needs to tell us at least once every day that we should overcome our fears. Fear is a lack of trust in our own ability and in God's forgiveness. Knowing that we are worth something helps us to overcome fear. Trust, more than anything, overcomes fear.

An anonymous quotation that I like is, 'We should fear less and hope more; we should eat less and chew more; we should hate less and love more and all good things will be yours.'

What kind of an 'eejit' are you?

5 August 2012

It's been a busy week. Far too busy. I had too many demands and after a long interview on the radio yesterday morning I felt so exhausted that I thought it was time to do a bit of thinking. So I went into the hospital to do a few visits and then came back and began to look through the week and some of the events which happened. I tried to learn something from them and asked myself a couple of questions. Where is God in any of the things I do?

Maybe a better question was that old one which we were forced to ask as young fellows playing football when we made a mistake – 'what kind of an eejit are you?'

So at my age when I should have my two feet up spending my life in retirement and only doing what I have to do, or want to do, I really do have to ask myself after the week I've had, what kind of an eejit am I?

I am not sure I will discover what kind of an eejit I am, but just come with me for part of my week anyway.

My first destination was Austria, but before that I attended a rally in support of a neighbouring family in Ballyconnell. It seemed to me to be a friendly, insignificant thing to do. But as you now know it's all the Press has had to talk about since. I learned the hard way that the old values are gone in Ireland. I never thought as a priest I would have to defend walking with neighbours. I did it when I was a year ordained, for a civil rights march. People asked me on that occasion what was a priest doing there? Forty-three years later when I walk with people they are still asking the same question. I learned that I have to be strong in standing up for what a priest should do. And that was why I explained on the radio yesterday that we still, in this part of the world, can love the sinner without condoning the sin. Whether people are right or wrong we still help them. None of us should be too quick to judge because we don't know which of us will need help before long.

Then I drove to Dublin, had an hour long meeting, got to bed for a couple of hours, got up in the middle of the night, was at the airport before five in the morning, got on a plane went to Austria and landed there at half past ten their time. At half past eleven we began filming and we finished filming just after seven in the evening. We had a quick bite to eat, went to bed and rose again at six the next morning to fly home and be ready for visiting the hospital and Mass here in Enniskillen on Tuesday evening.

What did I learn in Austria? There are four hundred priests there who have publicly said they will disobey the Vatican's orders on certain disciplines of the church. They will talk and ask about women priests. They will talk publicly about the need for married priests. They are refusing to take over five or six parishes because they recognise there are plenty of lay people in those parishes who could run them. They are refusing to say more than one Mass on a Sunday. For as long as they say more nobody will address the real issues. They will give Communion to people in second relationships if the people show themselves to be committed to each other and committed to their faith.

They have already been to Rome to speak with people in the highest circles including the Pope and indeed Pope Benedict spoke about them last Holy Thursday in pretty tough terms. But they are staying together as four hundred and not one of them has been silenced or censured yet. I wanted to know why and one of the main reasons, the priest told me was that the money which keeps the Vatican going comes from Austria and Germany. It made me even more cynical than before.

When I came home I discovered that people had been talking about me behind my back. But I also discovered that Maeve Binchy had died. Maeve was a lady I knew well and had many a good lunch with. She interviewed me and I interviewed her. Both of us told stories. There are many stories about Maeve but the one I like best was when she was a young editor of the women's page in *The Irish Times*. On a Saturday she had a cooking column by Theodora Fitzgibbons. Theodora was a precise lady whom I knew too and each week she would leave in an article of precisely six hundred and fifty words. Since her husband was a photographer there was usually a special picture left in too.

One Friday evening when Maeve was in a rush, Theodora left in her copy but there was no photograph. Maeve looked at the copy, read it through, passed it and then went to look for a photograph to go with the description of the meat dish which Theodora had described. As she looked through her files she saw a new picture which had come in of a beautiful piece of raw meat. She thought it would be a suitable picture for this piece and she sent it to the printers and went home.

That evening she was sitting with her father watching the 9 o'clock news. They were describing the very first heart transplant which had taken place that day by Professor Christian Barnard. The picture of the operation flashed up and to her horror Maeve recognised the picture. Instead of being a nice piece of meat with a knife and fork, what she had put in the cookery column was the picture of the heart transplant with a scalpel and grip. After a moment of panic she asked her father, who was a judge, what she should do. He told her to say nothing. She went outside, but couldn't find a taxi to take her from Dalkey to the centre of Dublin. She stopped a car and breathlessly told him she needed to get in to take a picture of a heart transplant out of a cookery column. She said, 'Are you going to the centre of Dublin?' He said he wasn't but he was now. He brought her in and the whole of *The Irish Times* was held up from printing. She eventually found a harmless picture of a Wedgwood egg cup. She put that in with the lines, 'precious food should always be eaten on Wedgwood'. Well as she tried to go home, exhausted, the editor called her into his office and gave her a severe telling off ending with the words, 'We could have become the first paper in the world to be sued for cannibalism.'

There was always a story. And always a redemption in Maeve's wonderful company.

When I opened my letters there was one from a man in Wicklow who enclosed €40 asking me to offer Mass for Marilyn Monroe, to mark the fiftieth anniversary of her death. He wrote that he thought no other priest in Ireland would do it. In fact most of them would laugh at him. But he thought I was the kind of guy who wouldn't mind offering a Mass for Marilyn Monroe and of course he was right.

There are lovely stories about Marilyn Monroe. She was no dumb blonde. She was the one who said, 'I don't think women should try to be equal to men – they should aim for something higher than that.'

Next day I was off to do some more interviews. One was with Mickey Harte. I asked him how his faith helped him through his difficulties. He began by telling me from whom he got his faith. The Hartes lived next door to the chapel. They looked after the chapel and took turns to do so. They were altar servers and they opened and closed the church each evening. When he got up each morning and looked out his window he saw a graveyard. So he was never afraid of death.

He knew all the prayers in Latin and in English. And each evening all the Harte family were gathered into the kitchen where they leaned on wooden chairs and said the Rosary. The family never questioned it. They just did it. And he said one of his most comforting moments ever was one evening when his father allowed him to sit on the chair which he was leaning on. He put his arms around him and his rosary beads dangled in front of him. He could feel the warm air of his father's breathe as he called the Rosary. Mickey says that was the most secure, godlike, safe moment in his life.

Mickey in turn taught his children to say the Rosary and they would always say it in the back of the car while they were travelling. Michaela, who was so cruelly murdered in Mauritius whilst on honeymoon, always said the Rosary on her way to and from work each day. It was her precious time, to think about God, and to offer the good and bad things of the day to God. Mickey said that without faith, he would never have the strength to go through what the family are enduring.

It is a pointer to us that faith is helpful and it doesn't have to be about rules and regulations. His father taught him that prayer itself isn't enough. You have to love your neighbours, be kind to them and help them to achieve their potential. A real practical form of daily living from Mickey Harte.

Yesterday I discovered another old friend Con Houlihan had died. Con was a wonderful journalist. He was a caring man who lived in Dublin all his life and he used to say: 'Kerry is my wife, but Dublin is my mistress.' He stood at matches and wrote the most beautiful prose. He had a first-class honours degree and was a doctor of the classics in Greek and Latin. He could quote them all, and English poetry too, in a report of a dull match. He wrote about the 'game of life', and used the game of football to illustrate it. He stood on the terraces with the rest of the people and never went to a press box.

His articles were written in big hand writing that could barely fit two paragraphs on the same page. But it was pure gold when it was transferred to a paper. We often walked to matches in Croke Park. He'd wait for me in Mountjoy Square and we'd chat on the way down. He had a Kerry accent which was difficult to understand. He asked me one day, 'Did you come down through Cavan?' I said I did. He said, 'Did you hear about the Cavan man who had a hip operation – he brought the bone home for the dog.' On another day he said, 'I bought a pair of shoes in Cavan last week, but they are very tight.'

We were together in Las Vegas in 1986 for Barry McGuigan's big fight against Stevie Cruz. It was one hundred and ten degrees and I was hardly able to walk in a shirt and trousers. But Con was there with a top coat, scarf, jacket, pullover, vest and God knows what else. He said when we came out of it one day: 'There's a great bit of heat today Brian. We should be at home winning the hay.' Con showed me that you can be yourself and be a genius.

As well as those things I went to three wakes and two funerals. I visited the hospital four times. Finally, I went to Derry to meet a group of people who are preparing a year of culture. And there I got a clue of how to put it all together. In a handwritten note from Seamus Heaney on a piece of paper I read:

> *So hope for a great sea change.*
> *On the far side of revenge.*
> *Believe that a farther shore*
> *Is reachable from here.*
> *Believe in miracles*
> *And cures and healing wells.*

And really isn't that what Jesus has said in the gospel today. 'I am the bread of life. He who comes to me will never be hungry. He who believes in me will never thirst.'

So at the end of all of that I don't really know what kind of an eejit I am. But I am happy to accept that to be an eejit is fine.

THAT *LATE LATE SHOW*

10 June 2012

I enjoyed the *Late Late* special, celebrating fifty years of the longest running chat show on television in the world. I met great friends that I hadn't seen in years – most of whom didn't have the opportunity to talk from the audience on the live show. It reminded me how important the *Late Late* is in Irish society. The *Late Late* has changed many a life, my own included.

During the programme Pat Kenny surprised everyone by skilfully recalling the famous confrontation between myself and the late Cardinal Daly in November 1995. It's now acknowledged as a turning point in the way senior clergy can expect to be treated. A valid opinion would not be suppressed by the might of the mitre. Pat linked it to my recent troubles with the Vatican. His insightful remarks were polite, positive and helpful.

I grew up watching the *Late Late* and was influenced by a wonderful Dominican priest, Fr Ferghal O'Connor. I first met Fr Ferghal when he lectured in UCD in Earlsfort Terrace. I followed his course in politics, and even after his course lectures were over, I, like dozens of others, never missed a lecture given anywhere by Fr O'Connor. He was simply brilliant. Looking back, he made me realise I should develop a mind of my own; he also gave me a method of thinking through problems, and then expressing an opinion, in a positive way.

Fr Ferghal often appeared on *The Late Late Show*. He was a real pioneer, speaking openly and honestly about matters of politics and society but mainly sexual morality. I discovered recently that the powers that be had repeatedly tried to silence him too. But he kept speaking in such a rational manner that he was never formally censured, even though he was often threatened. Through him, I learned how influential a man of integrity can be. He was probably the real reason why I debated with Cardinal Daly on that famous Late Late in 1995.

It all began accidentally enough. It certainly was not pre-planned. A week earlier, I had been in the canteen in RTÉ, when the then producer of *The Late Late Show*, John Masterson, asked me if I'd be part of the audience on the following Friday night's show which was, he told me, a special on the state of the Catholic Church in Ireland.

I told him I couldn't because I had already been booked by UTV for *The Gerry Kelly Show* on the same subject. But John insisted that there would be no conflict and so I agreed to attend. On the night itself I was recording a radio show for RTÉ 2FM and walked over to *The Late Late* just as the show was starting. There was no briefing and no preparation. Nobody told me who was going to be on the show or what issues were likely to come up.

Gay Byrne made the point on the fiftieth celebration show that quite frequently *The Late Late* was remembered, not for whole shows, but for small incidents that happened during a show. That is exactly how it panned out between myself and Cardinal Daly.

There had been a long discussion by many of the perceived influential people in Ireland both lay and clerical, about the state of the church. Halfway through, Cardinal Daly surprisingly was parachuted into the programme. He obviously hadn't picked up the hostile atmosphere and he proceeded to smile in all the wrong places, and say all the wrong things.

Mostly he repeated, 'We hear what you are saying, just go home and leave it to us.' That was his downfall. Everyone recognised the subplot. He was really telling us all that the hierarchy was in charge, we could have our night out on *The Late Late* but that in reality nothing was going to change.

The Late Late itself went into extra time. The final whistle was about to sound. But just then Gay looked over at me and nodded to me to make a comment. That's what makes Gay great. He didn't have a clue what I was going to say, but he read me and he knew by the expression on my face that I wouldn't hold back.

There wasn't much of a discussion really, it was a quick interchange but it had the effect of putting down the marker that even the Cardinal could be questioned live on television. When it was a matter as essential as protecting children, silence was no longer an option.

That was seventeen years ago. *The Irish Times* opined that 'Fr Trendy' was dead and that a more serious Brian D'Arcy had emerged. It was an inane comment and way off the mark. But that was how it was perceived. Thousands of people wrote and to this day I don't know whether I was right or wrong by challenging a man whom I knew and respected, Cardinal Daly.

What is important is that it certainly changed my life. *The Late Late Show* was then and still is a programme which people watch and remember. That's what makes it great. I hope it continues for many a long year to come.

Engaging People in
Decision Making

27 February 2011

A central problem facing churches all over the world is how to engage its members in meaningful decision making. Religions of all faiths are finding it difficult to wrestle control from their clerical leaders. It is not just the Catholic Church which is seriously clerical and where the all-male establishment refuses to allow other voices to be heard.

The problem was well addressed in a recent edition of *America*, which is the national catholic weekly published by the Jesuits. It had some novel suggestions as to how we might change church laws to ensure that laity, both men and women, can have a rightful say in the future of their church.

They based their arguments on what Jesus told his disciples – that they were to go into the world, feed the hungry, share their wealth with the poor, and have a practical love for one another. They were to offer their lives in service as he did with his.

As we know the culture of clericalism has practically destroyed the Catholic Church because it values its own peculiar form of loyalty above all other attributes including virtue and yet even a conservative Pope like John Paul II, quoting St Paulinus, admitted, 'Let us listen to what all the faithful say because in every one of them God's spirit breaths.'

America magazine like the rest of us has effectively given up hope of any change in the compulsory celibacy for priests law. We all know, that in the current climate, we are not even supposed to discuss the possibility of women's ordination. The church's inability to dialogue on both these issues is indefensible. Plainly there will not be a relaxation in compulsory celibacy nor will there be women priests in the immediate future. The church will be the poorer because of it and it runs the risk of becoming even more irrelevant.

We must not allow such obstinacy to lead to despair. There are other novel ways of allowing women and married men to use their talents in the service of the church, particularly in governing the church.

For example, a simple change in canon law could allow lay people, men and women, to become members of the College of Cardinals. Can you imagine what that would do? It would transform the all-male club into a community which resembles in some small way the people of God. The idea has been proposed ever since the Second Vatican Council which highlighted its possibility.

Now a less radical, but perhaps even more effective, proposal is to reorganise diocesan offices so that lay people constitute at least half of the bishop's advisors. We already have many good and efficient lay people working for the church. Without them we clerics simply couldn't carry on. It's a small step to involve them totally in all major decisions taken at diocesan and parish level. It should be their right, but clericalism is reluctant to relinquish power.

A really good idea to come out of the editorial in *America* magazine is to propose a new international council of lay people to share the functions of the College of Cardinals. 'After attrition among the cardinals, each of the two bodies eventually could have one hundred members,' the article proposed. It suggests a college of one hundred cardinals and a similar college of one hundred lay people, each with equal powers.

The lay people they say should be of sound Christian judgement and come from a wide variety of skills and occupations. They could be experts in education, health, religious life, law, the arts, business or medicine, etc. And they should be composed of men and women, married and unmarried.

We should never forget the contribution young lay people could make to the church. St Benedict recognised this over 1,500 years ago: 'By the Lord's inspiration it is often a younger person who knows what is best,' he wrote.

Like the editorial in the magazine, it would be wonderful to see lay people helping to administer the Vatican offices, advise the Pope and help select his successor. Now there's where real change might come.

Think of how more relevant the church's advice on contraceptives, the role of women in the church, the treatment of gay people and the failure of authority to act diligently on matters of clerical sexual abuse of children might become.

They might also have something to say about our liturgies, unprepared celebrants and boring sermons.

This is not a contradiction of what the papacy stands for. Pope John Paul II wrote: 'The authority proper to this ministry (Papacy) is completely at the service of God's merciful plan and it must always be seen in this perspective.'

That's the principle. Unfortunately in practice we still have a long way to go. Giving lay people the same power as elderly cardinals, could be the beginning of a revolution. It could happen and should happen, and maybe some day, by some miracle, it will happen.

'LOOK TO THE FUTURE WITHOUT FEAR'

I can reflect on the documentary *The Turbulent Priest* from a safe distance now. I have replied to all of the 1,200 people who contacted me by text, e-mail and letter. I have rarely been involved in anything which had almost unanimous support – with as little as half a dozen viewers expressing strong disagreement.

As Mary McAleese repeatedly points out, there is an educated and concerned laity who love the church and who are as dedicated to it, as any priest, bishop or canon lawyer and the church has not yet learned how to cope with them.

Since the programme was broadcast, I read again the magnificent address given at the opening of the Second Vatican Council on 11 October 1962 by Pope John XXIII. His inspired words refreshed my memory. The Council was a unique, graced time which changed the direction of the Catholic Church in a powerful way – if only the people in the Vatican had accepted Pope John's vision.

Pope John, in spelling out the purpose of the Council, expressed the hope that Vatican II would bless our church with new spiritual insights so that the church might 'look to the future without fear'.

If the faithful people could exercise the freedom Pope John initiated, there would be no need for sad documentaries. At the time, Pope John was hounded by the Vatican Civil Service. He was quite concerned about the unnamed officials who had a negative and pessimistic view of the world and of the church – and he didn't spare them. 'In the daily exercise of our pastoral office, we sometimes have to listen, much to our regret, to the voices of persons who, though burning with zeal, are not endowed with too much of discretion or measure,' he said.

Such statements today could have him on the censor's list. He referred to the curial officials as prophets of gloom, always forecasting disasters. It's hard to believe that the Pope had to suffer so much at the hands of the clerical civil service. Yet it is comforting to hear his straight-talking on the opening day of the Council.

He went on to express his own optimistic image for the future church. 'In the present order of things, divine providence is leading us to a new order of human relations ... which are directed toward the fulfilment of God's inscrutable designs. Everything, even human differences, leads us to the greater good of the church.' Those are the words of a confident open, humble pope who trusted the power of God's Spirit.

He was careful to safeguard the deposit of faith, but insisted that it was just as important to examine how the deposit of faith is communicated. He stated that the magisterium's role is to make the faith both known and reasonable for each new generation. Even more importantly, the teaching must be 'predominantly pastoral in character'.

It is inspiring just to read his words. That is precisely what so many are striving to do in today's church and in doing so find themselves hounded and threatened with expulsion from the active priesthood.

Pope John admitted that because we are human, errors come and go 'like the fog before the sun'. The church in the past, he went on, opposed errors with the greatest severity, but 'nowadays the spouse of Christ (the church) prefers to make use of the medicine of mercy rather than of severity ... she meets the needs of the present day by demonstrating the validity of her teaching rather than by condemnations.' What a beautiful expression of compassionate leadership.

Charity is at the centre of all renewal because nothing is as effective in 'eradicating the seeds of discord, nothing more efficacious in promoting concord, just peace and the unity of all,' John concluded.

For Pope John XXIII the spirit of the Vatican II church was shot through with hope and grounded upon the guidance of the Holy Spirit. In his church providence would banish fear and pessimism.

His opening address to the Council left us with a vision for the future: 'This council now beginning rises in the church like daybreak … It is now only dawn.'

That's the vision which gave my generation hope. I still believe that if we followed Pope John's advice, we could again be proud of our church.

CARDINAL MARTINI

9 September 2012

I was shocked and saddened to read that one of the most influential church leaders in Europe, Cardinal Mario Martini of Milan, expressly requested that his last interview should not be published until after his death. It beggars belief that such a senior churchman could be paralysed by fear – so much so that he wouldn't allow his true thoughts be known this side of the grave.

If his views were revolutionary, you might understand his fears. On the contrary his insights are shared by the vast majority of ordinary Catholics. The dying Cardinal wanted the world to know that in his opinion 'the church is two hundred years out of date'. Too many are too easily silenced by fear. Yet, he went on, we should be courageous because faith is the foundation of the church. Faith should give us the courage and the confidence to overcome fear.

'The church is tired in Europe and America. Our culture has aged, our churches are empty, our religious houses are empty and the bureaucracy of the church increases; our rituals and our clothes are pompous … We stand like the rich young man who went away sad when Jesus called him to make him a disciple,' he admitted.

The dying Cardinal revealed his frustrations in an interview with a fellow Jesuit, George Sporschill. The interview was 'a kind of spiritual testament' and was read and approved by Cardinal Martini some weeks before his death.

Cardinal Martini died at the age of eighty-five after a long illness. At one time he was everyone's favourite to replace John Paul II as Pope. Sadly he got Parkinson's disease but he still received a large number of votes at the conclave which elected Benedict XVI, before he withdrew his name because of ill-health.

The Cardinal's last interview has shocked those in power but has become a source of encouragement for those who long for renewal in the church. 'The church must admit its mistakes and begin a radical change, starting from the Pope and the bishops. The paedophilia scandals oblige us to take a journey of transformation,' he told the daily paper he wrote for, *Corriere della Sera*.

What is most disturbing is that a cardinal who could have become pope, who was a holy and revered scripture scholar and who was amongst the most respected church leaders in the world, felt he could not express his true convictions for fear of how the Vatican authorities might react. Obviously it is not just a few Irish priests who work under duress.

He proposed a threefold plan. Firstly there must be conversion which should 'follow a path of radical change … we must ask ourselves if people any longer listen to the advice of the church on sexual matters'.

Secondly we must immerse ourselves in the word of God. 'The Second Vatican Council returned the Bible to Catholics. Only the person who perceives in his heart this Word can be part of church renewal …'

Thirdly the sacraments are essential for healing and spiritual growth. 'The sacraments are not instruments of discipline but a help for people on their journey and in the weaknesses of life … are we carrying the sacraments to the people who need new strength?'

Agreeing that the church supports the indissolubility of marriage, he goes on to pose the question of what happens to a woman with children whose marriage breaks down and who meets a man who loves her and takes care of the children? 'If the parents are outside the church or do not feel the support of the church, the church will lose the next generation. Before receiving

Communion we pray 'Lord I am not worthy.' We know we are not worthy. Love is grace. Love is gift. The question of whether the divorced can take Communion should be turned around.' Those are the words the dying Cardinal used and approved.

Cardinal Martini was loved by his people. He understood their needs and spoke for them. Why then was he so afraid of 'the bureaucrats'? What has happened to Vatican II's all-embracing, 'People of God'? Where is Pope John XXIII's vision of respectful dialogue? What has become of our church?

What is clear is that priests and people together must be more resolved than ever to speak the truth with clarity and in charity; whatever the consequences I, and others like me, must take courage from Cardinal Martini's final, despairing plea for a renewed and relevant church. We owe it not only to the Cardinal, but to the church we love.

SECOND VATICAN COUNCIL

14 October 2012

On 11 October 1962 the wisest and most progressive Pope in recent history gathered more than two and a half thousand bishops from across the world with the special task of drawing up a blueprint for the future of religion in general and the Catholic Church in particular.

I remember the day well. I was a nervous young novice who had entered religious life five weeks earlier. I knew absolutely nothing about how the church worked but I had an idealistic commitment to give my life to God. The novice master told us we would have a day off on Thursday 11 October and that we could watch television. This was truly momentous for us because there was no television in the monastery. However a TV set was brought in so that we could join the whole community and watch a rolling black and white picture coming live from Rome. I had no idea at all of the significance of endless rows of stern looking men with pointy hats lined up waiting for the loveable and rotund Pope John XXIII to enter.

A year later, when I began to study theology, it dawned on me what a unique event this Second Vatican Council was. It could and should have had a mighty impact on the world and on belief itself.

The Second Vatican Council is often portrayed as an historical accident. It was anything but. Placed in context it was obvious that such a Council was inevitable. The destruction left by the Second World War, the Holocaust and millions of deaths, left the civilised world confused and looking for answers.

The world itself was changing at a faster rate than at any time in history. Communications were improving. There had been a worldwide ecumenical movement within the Protestant churches for close on forty years. The world just about survived the first nuclear explosion and was in danger of being destroyed completely by nuclear power. People were more educated and more articulate. The old structures of the world and of religion simply couldn't cope. Furthermore, Rome itself held preparatory discussions as far back as 1948.

For three years, when the Vatican Council met in ten-week blocks, there was an unprecedented surge of excitement. A new vision of the world and a new way to be religious in the world were clearly emerging. The documents themselves went far beyond what theologians expected. The miracle of the Holy Spirit giving new life to some of the most traditional bishops was astounding.

The careerists in the Roman Curia initially produced documents which reflected their view of the world. The bishops, with the encouragement of Pope John XXIII, rejected almost everything they produced and set about writing new documents tackling vital problems for their peoples in the remotest parts of the world. The Curia's view of the world was not what the Pope or rest of the bishops wanted.

Fifty years later the excitement, enthusiasm and probably the spiritual impact of the council, have waned. As a result large numbers have walked away from religion, particularly the Catholic religion. In most cases the wonderful documents are largely forgotten.

There are many reasons why this has happened – all of them rooted in human nature. To begin with we now know that documents in themselves do not produce change. They may produce a plan for change but they do not give us a destination. Human nature resists such change.

Documents, no matter how radical, need people of conviction to put them into practice. One of the great tragedies was that the clerics in positions of power within the Vatican were able to resist the changes and effectively smother the work of the Council.

Ladislas Örsy, one of the last surviving participants of the Second Vatican Council, along with pioneering theologians like Frs Yves Congar, John Courtney Murray and Henri de Lubac, wrote the magnificent documents of the Second Vatican Council. Congar, Courtney Murray and De Lubac were all silenced by the Vatican during the 1950s but re-emerged as the prophets of the new church under John XXIII.

Fr Örsy is still optimistic that the work of the Holy Spirit cannot be frustrated forever. He compares it to a tsunami which cannot be stopped. He reminds us that Pope John XXIII was himself an old school theologian who learned during the Council to leave aside certainties and trust the Holy Spirit. The Pope constantly reminded us that the council opened the windows of the stuffy old church to let in the fresh air of God's Spirit. The church should not be a museum preserving the past, but a beautiful garden full of life and hope and vision.

The Council itself said that the Holy Spirit 'hovers over the whole human family' and that the church must continually recognise goodness wherever it is found within the human family.

The council produced its own special vocabulary. One of the most used words was *aggiornamento* which leads to an openness to communicate the Good News to the whole world. Pope John XXIII described the Council as 'a new Pentecost which would give life and hope to the lonely and lost everywhere'.

Maybe that's why I am finding a new enthusiasm within myself as I read again the documents of the Second Vatican Council. The world has changed but the principles laid down in the main documents are still exciting and exhilarating. The church is the people of God. If we can wrestle our church back from suffocating institutionalism then there may still be a hopeful future. Ladislas Örsy is correct: 'Nothing can be more alienating to the mind of the council than a church withdrawn into an enclave ... the energy of the Holy Spirit will prevail ... there is no way of stopping it ... they have no power to stop it.'

DOUBTS

16 December 2012

In recent months I've had a few setbacks in my life and they chipped away at my confidence and, worse still, my peace of mind. So this is an opportune time to give myself a good talking to.

Life has taught me that I cannot think myself into a new way of living; rather I have to live myself into a new of thinking. I have to discover what works for me and that will help to change my thinking about myself.

I am often preoccupied about where my life is going. Does my priestly ministry make a blind bit of difference to anyone? Perhaps I'm doing more harm than good. Such self-doubt is normal enough, but it needs to be dealt with, otherwise it will destroy everything I do.

That is why I must work hard to deal with issues instead of suppressing them. This is normal healthy living. It's when issues are laughed at or worse still denied, that real hypocrisy takes over.

Mahatma Gandhi was convinced that a person becomes what they believe themselves to be. 'If I keep on saying to myself that I cannot do a certain thing,' Gandhi wrote, 'then I will become incapable of doing it. But if I have the belief that I can do it, I shall surely acquire the capacity to do it.' I think he was right.

So, frequently now I take time to reflect. I hide away in a quiet corner to allow God into my life. Recently the strangest thought came to me. 'Even the hairs of your head have been counted' – which is a saying of Jesus, recorded in St Luke's Gospel (Lk 12:1). Within minutes I felt better about my life.

It was like someone telling me: You matter. Your life has meaning; every hair of your head is counted – you have nothing to fear, for God sees everything you do. That's when the name of basketball coach John Wooden came to my mind. He put it so well: 'Success comes from knowing that you did your best to become the best you are capable of becoming.'

FORGIVENESS

1 May 2011

Forgiveness is one of those subjects which is alright for others to practice, but doesn't apply to how I live my own life.

It's often said that forgiveness is for 'religious' people. That's rubbish. Forgiveness is for everyone who wants to lead a healthy, emotional life. Psychology and theology have studied the value of forgiveness for hundreds of years. Psychology defines forgiveness as 'the process of ceasing to feel resentment, indignation or anger against another for a perceived or real offence'.

These days psychology and psychiatry have invented their own rituals of forgiveness. Mostly they borrow formulae from religions. They know that anyone who gets stuck in a manure pit of bitterness, will never live in peace. No tablet will heal jealousy or anger.

Victims often conclude that it they forgive the one who hurt them, they also excuse them. Victims mistakenly think they have to forget the injuries they suffered as part of the forgiveness process. Not so! To forgive somebody is to leave their actions with them. They must still face themselves. They have to live with the consequences. They have to deal with their own guilt.

If we have been victimised in a serious way, we can never forget it. But because we can't forget, doesn't mean we can't free ourselves; that we can't offer the healing balm of forgiveness to ourselves.

Forgiveness does not remove culpability. The perpetrator is always responsible for his/her actions.

It was Shakespeare in *The Merchant of Venice* who wrote, 'Forgiveness is twice blest. Blessed is him that gives and him that takes.'

The person who cannot forgive at all is the unhealthiest one of all. Studies in religion and psychology have shown that those who have the capacity to forgive tend to have healthy, emotional lives. They have a lower rate of stress-related illnesses and have better interpersonal relationships. It doesn't matter whether the forgiveness comes through religion or through psychiatry, the results are the same, peace of mind.

Sometimes we need help to journey through the forgiveness process. When it's successful it's the best present you can give yourself. Offering forgiveness is a quality to admire but it is also a quality which gives great benefits to the one who forgives.

Important Stories

11 November 2012

I was at an Association of Catholic Priests meeting in Dublin on Friday night. There were a lot of discussions – it wasn't well attended. There were about three to four hundred in all and it was about half and half, lay people and priests. Obviously there were discussions about how we can have a church that lives in the real world and which treats its citizens with respect. One woman decided that she would tell a story which might highlight a point to meditate on.

It began with a woman visiting Rome. She was tired after a day's sightseeing and sat down at a kerbside café to have a little coffee. She overheard three men with Irish accents speaking. The first talked about how wonderful it was to be in Rome. He was so proud that he had a son, a priest. 'When he comes into a room everybody calls him Father, stands up and he's like a father to the community.'

The second man said, 'Well I can understand that because my son is a bishop and when he comes into a room everybody stands up, calls him My Lord, kisses his ring and moves out of his way while he puts on his mitre and vestments.'

The third said, 'All of those are wonderful privileges but my son is a cardinal and he's a young cardinal and when he comes into a room everybody stands up and calls him Your Eminence. I was thinking that he's so young that he could be at the election of two or three popes in his lifetime.'

They all agreed that being in Rome and having a family member in the priesthood was great. They looked over to the woman who was listening intently. 'Have you a son in the priesthood?' she was asked. She replied, 'I don't have any sons. But I've three daughters. And the youngest of them is twenty-three. She's tall; she's blonde; she's shaped like an hourglass has wonderful, long, well-formed legs. And when she walks into a room in a mini-skirt, even the Cardinal stands up and says, 'Oh my God.'

Women do have power.

Stories are important. I remember an American colleague who was a bright theologian visiting Ireland. He was the kind of man who was developed from the neck up but not so developed from the neck down. He was an intellectual.

I brought him to see St Kevin's Bed in Glendalough in Wicklow. I tried to tell him some of the myths, legends and stories about St Kevin. I explained that his cell was tiny that once when Kevin was preparing his dinner he decided to pray. He knelt down and stretched his arms out in the shape of a cross. To do that he had to put each arm out through windows in the side of his little round cell. Whilst he was praying he got into such a trance that when he came to he discovered that a blackbird was building a nest in his hand. St Kevin prayed until the blackbird built the nest, laid her eggs, hatched her chickens and until they were able to fly. Kevin never moved but held his arms in the shape of a cross till the blackbird completed its work. Then he made his dinner. From now on we'll call it the Glendalough diet. It is foolproof.

My theologian friend looked at me and said, 'That's nonsense.' I explained to him that from one point of view it was nonsense. But the point of a story is that it doesn't matter if it's factual or not. What's the point of this story? Anyone who had moved from their head to their heart would understand that the point of the story is that in Kevin's spirituality all creation is important. All creation is of service to each other part of creation. That however is a language that science doesn't understand. It's the language of the heart which really knows what a story is about.

The stories of the two widows in today's readings are part of that same tradition. Initially we meet the widow from Sidon who was so exhausted from famine that she was about to die. Elijah, the prophet, came in God's name and asked her to share what she had. She said she had only a handful of meal in a jar and a little oil in a jug. She was gathering the sticks to prepare a fire so that she could bake what little she had for herself and her son before they died.

Elijah assured her that she had no need to fear. She should make a scone for him and there would be plenty for her son. The woman did as Elijah told her out of faith. They ate the food, all three, and there was plenty of meal and oil left over. Those who trust the Lord will never walk alone.

Likewise we have the story of the widow in the gospel. It is contrasted with the first half of the gospel where the leaders of the religion of the time had got themselves so caught up in show for the sake of show that they had lost sight of the reason for their existence. Not so the widow.

The treasury was a vessel to collect money for the upkeep of the temple. It was made of metal, when the coins dropped into it astute people knew exactly what was put into the vessel by the sound of the coin dropping.

The rich put in plenty from what they had left over and the priests and leaders of the church were pleased by this. The poor widow threw in two coins which everybody recognised as the smallest coin in existence. She was the one who was noticed by Jesus. He called the disciples and said, 'If you want somebody to imitate when you become leaders in our church forget about the people dressed in robes looking for money. Rather look at that widow. She's the one who's closest to me because she does exactly what I do. She gives everything she has. I would give my last drop of blood. She would give her last possession in this world.'

Sometimes we talk about the widow's mite as if it was little. But Jesus points out that she is an extravagant woman. The others give from their plenty but she gives everything, even though she has little to give. The widow tells us that the value of a gift is determined not by how it seems in the receiver's mind, but what it costs the giver. The mite is not a measure of money; the mite is a measure of love and trust.

Fr Peter McVerry said that compassion is the greatest gift we can give and the one which is the most lacking in the world today. He points out that if we are to show the God of compassion to the world then we must become the compassion of God to the needy. The extent to which we love God, he says, can be measured by the limit of our love for those we love least. Think of someone that you hardly love at all and that'll be a good measure of our love for God.

It's a bit like the judge in Cavan settling a divorce case. After sitting a long time he gently came to his conclusion and told the husband, 'I am going to give your wife £1,000 a month.' To which the Cavan man said, 'That's very good of you, Your Honour, and seeing that you're so generous, sure I might throw her a few pound myself.'

Different to that was St Paul who said, 'God loves a cheerful giver.' True generosity is not measured by how much we give, but by how much we have left.

SPRINGTIME

25 April 2010

If you want to make God laugh tell him your plans. That was a thought which came to my mind as I went out for my early morning meditation/walk. This year spring is late. April is a time when nature is barely awakening from its winter slumber. As I walked along the country roads and saw signs of buds and flowerings, it was easy to know that God is rising to new life in nature. The words of Patrick Kavanagh came to mind:

> *Oh give me faith*
> *that I may be*
> *alive when April ecstasy*
> *dances in every whitethorn tree.*

There were thorn blossoms in bloom but I am reliably told they were the white blossoms of blackthorns. The birds were chirping and I stopped to listen as God spoke to me in the silence of the countryside, in the new clothes that nature was putting on hedges and ditches, in petals dropping off the trees almost like snow and in shy primroses making the grass look green again after its winter scorching.

My favourite oak tree seems to be enjoying its own resurrection. It was easy to pray, 'O give me faith, that I may be alive when April's ecstasy dances in every whitethorn tree.'

As I walked I began to question myself gently. Am I really alive? Have I left the past behind? Am I willing to risk and trust so that I can have a future? Am I willing to believe that God is still walking with me? Have I any life left within me?

Many of us who are professional religious people, choose to remain in the past to be comfortable, rather than risk a future for ourselves. Most of us in fact are more comfortable choosing death than we are choosing life. Yet the gospel stories after the Resurrection ask the most important question of all: 'Why look for the living among the dead?'

Whatever about the desperate failings of the institutional church, it's time for the rest of us to move to new places and to minister to the real world. It's time to accept the challenge, to make God present in the world in a way that is gentle and saving. It may mean leaving much-loved buildings, places and structures behind. Our mission is not about any of those things – it's about a message of hope for those who need it; a message of peace for the troubled; a message of life for those who flounder under the weight of outdated structures.

When I came to offer Mass, the gospel summed it up. The disciples, who had betrayed and denied Jesus, were asked one simple question. 'Do you love me?' It wasn't about confession or repentance or humiliation. Love conquers everything, including sin.

Our God is more interested in our future prospects than in our past failures. Our God is disgusted by abuse and by those who covered up. Our God is greater than the puny efforts of clerical clubs and criminals and sinners.

So relieved, I stepped into the refreshing shower and as I was shaving I told myself, 'If I can still love, I am still alive.'

LISTEN TO THE PEOPLE

30 September 2012

It's no secret that people all over the world are leaving organised religion. To ask why people are leaving the Catholic Church is seen to be disloyal and will be seen to reprimand from on high.

Bishop O'Connell of Trenton, New Jersey, took a more positive approach and hired a professional group to dialogue with Catholics who have made a conscious decision to stay away from weekly Eucharist. In all they interviewed three hundred absentees over an extended period and the survey revealed some enlightening trends. It was compiled by William J. Byron, a Jesuit priest.

The researchers discovered that an overwhelming number of the respondents left both their parish and their church. About a quarter said they had separated themselves from the parish but still considered themselves to be Catholics. 'I separated my family from the Catholic Church and turned to an alternative religion for a while and then returned knowing that I had the right religion but the wrong people running it,' one woman wrote.

Relatively few drifted away. The vast majority had sincerely tried to make their membership of the church a rewarding spiritual experience but gave up in frustration.

A twenty-three-year-old woman wrote, 'I felt deceived and undervalued by the church. I didn't understand certain things and found no mentors within the church. I stopped going because my community of friends and family were no longer in the church.'

And another added with great clarity, 'I tried different Catholic churches in the area because I just didn't seem to be getting anything out of Mass, especially the homily.' That was a common theme, also well expressed by this respondent: 'I stopped going regularly because the homilies were so empty and whenever the church wanted to raise funds, they dropped the homily and talked money.'

As you would expect, the scandal of the sexual abuse of minors by clergy was frequently mentioned. Equally damaging was the way the crisis was handled by the leadership in the church.

The interviewees were asked, 'Are there any changes your parish might make that would prompt you to return?' The researchers found no discernible trend in the replies but people are willing to enter dialogue if they are convinced they will be taken seriously. Here are some of the issues they want to discuss:

* Be accepting of divorced and remarried congregants.

* A desire for more spiritual guidance and longer sermons.

* Make homilies more relevant; give us an outwardly loving, kind, Christian priest/pastor.

By a margin of two to one respondents reported that they did at one time consider being part of a parish community. Those who left felt that they were no longer part of a community. 'I did not experience community in the sense that I knew people just from going to church. The ones I knew, I knew them outside the church. No one missed us when we stopped going. No one called from the parish even though we were regular attenders and envelope users.'

As part of the discussion the people were asked, 'Are there any religious beliefs/practices specific to the Catholic Church that troubled you?' Here is a sampling of what people replied:

* Yes, the church's views on gays, same-sex marriage, women as priests and priests not marrying.

- History of discrimination against women, unwelcoming attitude.

- Bishops covering up child abuse and transferring offending priests to other parishes.

- End the clericalism and people like me may listen to the church again.

- If the Catholic Church does not change its archaic views about women, it is going to become a religion that survives on the fringes of an open-minded, progressive society.

All of the above were seen as helpful by the Bishop of Trenton, his staff and researchers.

Fr Byron concluded that there was much to be learned from the survey. The obligation to attend Sunday Mass needs further explaining. The quality of preaching in churches needs attention as does the image of clergy who – fairly or unfairly – are often seen as distant, unavailable and uncaring.

There were many other issues raised which were helpful. You will find them on the website of the Diocese of Trenton, New Jersey. The best sign of hope for me was that people were willing to share their opinions in such a positive way.

CHRISTIAN UNITY

29 January 2012

The Week of Prayer for Christian Unity has been a part of the church's calendar for more than one hundred years. According to the *Atlas of Religion*, Christianity is the world's largest religion. It has more than 2.1 billion followers. It's hard to believe though, that there are almost thirty-four thousand Christian denominations in two hundred and thirty-eight different countries. The vast majority belong to six major Christian traditions, though well over four hundred million are affiliated to independent Christian churches. A sense of unity and community is more crucial than ever. That's why Christian Unity Week is important.

The French theologian Paul Couturier summed up its aim succinctly: 'We must pray, not that others may be converted to us, but that we may all be drawn closer to Christ.'

In forty years of ministry, the most hopeful change that has taken place for me is the respect, and understanding, which has grown up among the main Christian churches. Unity among Christians is both a challenge and a necessity, if our churches are to be relevant in a changing world.

John Wesley who was the founder of the Methodist Movement, visited Ireland twenty-one times. On one of his last visits, he was so appalled by the hatred that existed between Protestants and Catholics that he wrote a letter to both groups advising that, as Christians, they should take a number of simple steps to improve relations. They should resolve not to hurt one another; to make sure to say nothing harsh or unkind about each other's beliefs; to harbour no unkind or unfriendly thoughts towards each other and lastly, 'to help each other in whatever way we are agreed leads to the Kingdom [of God]'.

In that context, I must admit that for many years I thought the Week of Prayer for Christian Unity was a waste of time. At best it seemed to me to be little more than window dressing. But I don't think that way anymore.

For the last twenty-two years my ministry has been in Northern Ireland, and I know how effective Christians working and praying together has been. When Christian leaders first began to work alongside one another, there was a silent undercurrent of bigotry, which allowed the more sinister elements to run a campaign of hate. During those years of violence almost four thousand people lost their lives and countless other thousands were damaged physically and emotionally. Yet in the midst of such strife, Christians came together to pray, to work for justice, and to oppose violence.

I believe that Christian Unity is most effective when it's built on respect – respect for ourselves, and a healthy respect for difference.

Christian Unity isn't simply about a comfortable notion of friendliness and co-operation. It requires a willingness to dispense with competition between us. All we have is gifted to us by Christ and the only true victory is to use our gifts for the glory of God's Kingdom. There is room for everyone in God's plan of salvation.

JUDGEMENTS

18 November 2012

A kind gentleman sent me this story and I think there is a certain amount of truth in it. It is a conversation between a 10p coin and a £10 note. Both of them found themselves in the dark recesses of a man's pocket. The £10 began to boast about all the places he'd been. 'I've a great life. I'm only three years old but I've been to Spain, France, London; I've been in some of the best restaurants in the country; and I'm regularly in the best pubs in the country. It's always exciting to look forward to where I'm going next. What about you?' The 10p coin began, 'Well the only place I'm certain I'm going to is heaven. I haven't been to very many places in my life. In fact the only place that I appear regularly is in the church collection. So with all of that religion at least I should get to heaven.' And the coin could be right.

The church is often out of step with the world. The end of the church year is next Sunday. On the first Sunday of December we begin a new year in Advent. On these Sundays we're urged to review our spiritual life. We're clearly urged today to get our life in order, lest death catch us unawares. People in this part of the country seem to enjoy talking about death. At my brother's wake a man approached me; he looked at Gaby's remains and he looked at me and he gave me a wee nudge. With great seriousness he said, 'They're beginning to take them off our shelf now, Fr Brian.' That's just what you don't want to hear at that time.

I visited the hospital the other day and met a man who had been admitted that day. He was quite at ease in the bed and he repeated another truism when he said, 'It's true what they say.

You can put on your own boots in the morning but you don't know who'll take them off.' It's a bit pessimistic but there's also a certain truth in it. That's exactly what the readings are doing today. They're a bit pessimistic but you can't argue with them.

When I was young the idea of thinking about the last judgement was part of our life. The sermons were often about heaven and hell and what happens when we die. My mother taught me to say a perfect Act of Contrition every night before I went to bed. If you went to Confession an *imperfect* Act of Contrition would do but without the sacrament we needed a *perfect* Act of Contrition. Don't ask me what the difference is and don't ask me how you could say an imperfect Act of Contrition. Either you're sorry or you're not sorry, either you intend to sin again or you don't. But that's the way it was.

I imagined myself as a young, skinny boy from Bellanaleck with my two hands in my pockets standing before God and all the neighbours gathered around. God will say, 'This man's a sham. Here are all the lies he told; here are all the biscuits he stole; here's all the times he didn't say his prayers; here's all the times he was disrespectful while he was celebrating Mass.' I felt uncomfortable and began to make sure I did things correctly lest when I'd be exposed before the nation I'd be a total hypocrite.

As I grow older though I think much less about judgements. I try to convince myself that God does indeed love me. If I'm convinced that God loves me unconditionally then everything else is insignificant. It's easier to beat yourself up than to accept God's love even though you don't deserve such love. I think less and less about judgements, I simply try not to be afraid and to accept God's love.

C.S. Lewis was a wonderful writer and philosopher. The film *Shadowlands* was about his life. He was a thoughtful, religious man, later in life especially. He had an admirer named Joy Davidson who came from America to live in England. Her marriage had just broken up and she arrived with her children. She became infatuated with Lewis who was known as Jack all his life, after he became overly concerned with grief when his dog Jack died. Ever afterwards he was called Jack. But Joy contracted cancer and in the face of cancer he realised how much he loved her. He overcame all his impediments and asked her to marry him. They had a lovely, romantic time and quite frequently in their conversations Joy would remind Jack, 'It's not going to last, Jack.' He would become disconsolate and say, 'Let's enjoy what we have while we have it and don't think of the future.' But she answered wisely, 'To think about it doesn't spoil it Jack, it makes it real. The pain is part of our happiness now.' I think that's a wonderful insight.

Daniel tells us that no matter what happens we should hold on, stay faithful and be loyal. Jesus on the other hand is talking to his disciples, seventy-two hours before his death, in the Mount of Olives, the very place where he'd suffered the agony in the garden. He gave this farewell speech to his disciples to tell them that he was not the Messiah they were anticipating. A loyal father who will give the same reward to them for being loyal and faithful as he has given to Jesus himself.

The fig-tree is one of the few trees in the Holy Land which loses its leaves. So he took that as an example. We know when it's naked it has lost its leaves but we also know that in the spring those leaves will come again. We need to be able to read the signs of the times. Live life fully, that is our best preparation for death. Everything changes and each of us, as we grow older, realises the world we grew up in has passed on. We have to be able to recognise God's plan for us in an ever-changing world.

We have to be able to make the best of things. Adlai Stevenson once wrote, 'Journalists separate wheat from weeds and then throw away the wheat.' I think he was right when he said that. We, too, do the same. We get overly-concerned about the dross and the weeds of life and all the things that don't matter. Then we throw away the precious pearls that are gifted to us. Heaven and earth will pass away 'and we should learn to hold on to what matters'.

Mark Twain said, 'Some people are bothered about the bits of the Bible they don't know. I'm bothered about the pieces I do know.'

WORDS OF WISDOM

12 February 2012

Too much choice is a bad thing. It is easier for me to pass on wisdom to others than it is for me to live by my own wisdom. I became aware of this insight when I was trying to comfort a woman in hospital who was close to death. She was finding it difficult to find peace – mainly because she could forgive everyone else their faults, but was tortured by her own failures. She asked me to share a short prayer which might help her to cope with her troubled past, in the dark hours of the lonely night.

I tried to keep it simple, to make it meaningful enough to penetrate her morphine state of mind. I whispered: 'Lord help me to realise that I am not as good as I ought to be, and to be thankful that I am not as bad as I used to be.' She seemed pleased, and, as I backed out of the room, I could see her calmly mouthing some of the words.

On my way back to see her the following morning, I wondered if the prayer had helped to ease her troubled mind. Sadly, the nurses told me that she had died shortly after I left the hospital, so I'll never know.

Since then I've begun to use the words as a kind of mantra for myself. It was easy for me to pass on words of comfort to her, but did I really believe those words myself? I have to face up to the fact that I need to live a more dedicated life; I am not perfect, never will be perfect, but actually I don't need to be perfect. That's the point. So, 'Lord help *me* to know that I am not as good as I ought to be, and to realise that I am not as bad as I think I am.'

To paraphrase the wise words of author James Baldwin about the problems of life: 'Not everything that is faced can be changed, but nothing can be changed until it is faced.'

ALL SAINTS

30 October 2011

Since the eighth century, the celebration of the feast of all the saints of the church, both known and unknown, has been observed by the western church on 1 November. Before that it was celebrated on the first Sunday after Pentecost.

I've lived with a few saints in various monasteries in my lifetime, though they certainly wouldn't have said so themselves! They were invariably quiet men who prayed when it was appropriate and who selflessly ministered to people in need, without looking for recognition or thanks. The one outstanding quality each of them had, was an openness to doing God's will even when it didn't suit them. In contrast, the men who made a fuss of appearing 'holy' did what suited themselves and nothing more.

I've also been privileged to minister to a few saints in the places where I've worked. One who comes to mind was Mary who, when her husband died, decided to foster very young babies. She devoted her life to these little innocents who were vulnerable, delicate and awaiting a more permanent home. They often had to be fed during the night and I doubt if Mary had an uninterrupted night's sleep for the twenty years she did the work.

A few years ago I met another special 'saint'. She was a young, bright, gorgeous person who suffered from spina bifida. She accepted her illness totally and on the nights I was called to her home when she couldn't breathe, she had the courage to thank God for her blessings. She died peacefully and unexpectedly one night before she reached her twentieth birthday. Before she died she told her mother not to worry because she said she, 'could see God on the other side'. In all probability none of these good people will be formally canonised by the church which is why we need All Saints Day to honour not just the heralded but those unheralded members of our community.

The scripture scholar Denis McBride has a telling quote about All Saints and All Souls. He writes, 'We rejoice in the saints we have known and know; their name is legend. We bless God for those who attend to the hungry, the orphans, the aged, the lepers, the outcasts, and the overlooked. We thank God for those who have out-smiled the jibes and taunts of oppressors; for those whose whispered prayers have enriched the holiness of us all; for those who struggle honestly against ending up selfish and unloving. We express our gratitude for those whose lives are welcomed as good news by the poor, for those who confront religious pretence. For those who keep on forgiving with an energy that is worthy of God. For these people, among us still, we give thanks.'

Oscar Wilde had a word for almost every occasion. This is what he said about saints. 'The only difference between a saint and a sinner is that every saint has a past and every sinner has a future.'

In more recent times, Sidney Harris put it succinctly when he wrote, 'The saint loves people and uses things. The sinner loves things and uses people.'

All Saints Day helps to assure us that if we remain true to God's calling we will some day see God as God really is. The First Letter of St John has these comforting words: 'Think of the love that the father has lavished on us, by letting us be called God's children; and that is what we are.'

All Saints is a reminder to us also that holiness is not the monopoly of any particular religion or tradition. Wherever there are good people trying to make the world a better place to live in, then God is working through them.

Shortly after he became President of South Africa, there were many people calling Nelson Mandela a saint. When I met him for a short interview it was the first question I put to him. 'President

Mandela, are you a saint?' Just as quickly he gave me his answer. 'I have no idea what a saint is. I have heard it said though, that a saint is a sinner who tries harder. If that is so,' he chuckled, 'then I am a saint.'

EUNICE KENNEDY SHRIVER

26 August 2012

Years ago when the remains of a famous woman were brought to the church the family gathered around her casket. As they waited there a twenty-five-year-old special needs man called Mike Rhodes placed a card on the casket. It was one he himself had made. When the family opened it, his barely legible writing said, 'She taught us all to stand tall.' What a magnificent legacy for any person to leave.

That woman was Eunice Kennedy Shriver, who founded the Special Olympics, which in turn brings life, joy, dignity and a chance to be different to millions of disadvantaged athletes – as we always see when the Paralympics are held.

I never met Eunice Kennedy Shriver but I have met members of her family. I met her mother Rose. Rose was a formidable lady who went to Mass every day, prayed the Stations of the Cross after it and then recited the Rosary. She had nine children who did great good throughout the world and some of whom also lived destructively too. I met Ted Kennedy more than once. I found him an approachable man with a brilliant brain. He knew Northern Ireland inside out. I also had a meal with Eunice's, sister Jean Kennedy Smith, who served as US ambassador to Ireland.

Eunice died as a result of a stoke at eighty-eight years of age. In her life she had many claims to fame. She was a sister to President John F. Kennedy and Senator Robert Kennedy, who was murdered in the same manner as the President. Senator Robert took on the mafia and paid the price. Her husband ran as a vice-presidential candidate and her daughter Maria Shriver was one of the most famous of all TV personalities before she met and married Arnold Schwarzenegger, the former Governor of California.

Yet Senator Ted Kennedy once said about his sister Eunice, 'If the test of a successful life is to be determined by what has helped humanity, then no other member of the Kennedy family has done more than Eunice.' He went on to say that Eunice understood better than any of the rest of the family what her parents had taught them, 'Much is expected from those to whom much has been given.'

Time magazine said that she led a social revolution which eventually changed not only attitudes, but laws, expectations and opportunities.

She founded the Special Olympic Games which do so much to bring children with special needs to the forefront of society. Her sister Rosemary was special needs. Eunice was the middle of nine children and was closest in age to Rosemary. They played together; they became very close. Rosemary eventually had to be committed to an institution after a brain operation went wrong. But Eunice knew that swimming in the pool, playing games and allowing Rosemary to do the things the rest of the family did, made Rosemary a happy, fulfilled and valued person. It ran contrary to the wisdom of the time which said that the mentally disadvantaged should not be encouraged to exercise because it was too trying for them.

In 1968, a few weeks after her brother Bobby had been assassinated, she organised and financed the first Special Olympics for special needs athletes. It took place in Soldier Field, Chicago. There were one thousand athletes from twenty-six States present. When the games came to Ireland in 2003, six thousand five hundred athletes from one hundred and fifty countries took part.

Then she brought the Special Olympics to China which had a record of intolerance towards those with mental disability. The Chinese Government had to welcome the seven thousand athletes and their families from one hundred and sixty countries who went to China.

Today the worldwide organisation for the Special Olympics helps, on an ongoing basis, over two million special needs people.

The family of Eunice Shriver summed it up perfectly when they said, 'She set out to change the world and to change her children. She did both. She taught us by example and by passion what it means to live a faith-driven life of love and service to others.' That's what real spirituality leads to – making the love of God present in others' lives.

To finish off I want to tell you my favourite story from the Special Olympics. At the Seattle Special Olympics, nine contestants, all physically or mentally disadvantaged, assembled at the starting line of what was to be a one hundred yards contest.

At the gun they all started out, not exactly in a dash, but with enthusiasm to run the race to the best of their ability and hopefully win. All, that is, except for one little boy who stumbled on the track, tumbled over a few times and began to cry.

When the other eight heard the boy cry, they slowed down to find out what was wrong.

Then they all turned around and went back … every single one of them.

One little girl with Down's Syndrome bent down and kissed him and said, 'This will make it better.'

Then all nine linked arms and walked together to the finishing line. Everyone in the stadium stood cheering.

The one thing that should matter in life is helping others win even if it means changing course ourselves.

TAKE THE PLUNGE

27 May 2012

Two of the best writers and thinkers on the future of religion today are Archbishop Rowan Williams and Fr Timothy Radcliffe. One is Anglo-Catholic and the other is Roman Catholic.

Timothy Radcliffe holds a unique position in the modern Catholic Church. Formerly Master of the Dominican Order in Rome for nine years, he was one of the most influential leaders in the Catholic Church. He is also a gifted writer and speaker.

In his book *Take the Plunge: Living Baptism and Confirmation*, he explores the background to Baptism. His aim is to help us begin to rediscover its meaning, the privileges it confers, and the responsibilities it demands. About a third of the world's population is baptised – that is to say 2.3 billion people – yet it is fair to say few, if any of us, live up to the challenges baptism presents.

There are many wonderful quotations which lighten the journey through Fr Radcliffe's profound book. The main theme is that Christianity will survive only insofar as we rediscover the beauty of baptism. 'It touches the deepest dramas of human life, of growing up, falling in love, daring to give oneself to others, searching for meaning, coping with suffering and failure and eventually death.'

Fr Timothy's humour helps unlock the significance of baptism. He writes, 'Jesus calls to his friend; "Lazarus come out," (John 11, 43).' I wished to use that quote as a title for a talk in Los Angeles, but I was discouraged in doing so on the grounds that it might suggest that Lazarus was gay.'

It's a quote I have often used myself yet never thought of the possible implications. I did however know that Bertrand Russell, the famous atheist philosopher, once said, 'The Ten Commandments should be treated like an examination paper; no candidate should attempt more than six.' He has a point, but Jesus actually reduced all law to one commandment in three parts – 'Love the Lord your God with all your heart; love your neighbour and love yourself.'

Fr Radcliffe writes: 'It is the vocation of the baptised to speak good, healing, blessing-filled words. We are called to purify the words of even their implicit poison, the little unhelpful metaphors that lurk unnoticed.'

I remember as a student attending lectures given by Fr Herbert McCabe, another brilliant Dominican, who spoke in Dublin in the mid 1960s. Back then, I understood about a tenth of what he said. Yet it was enough to put a fire in my belly.

McCabe visited South Africa in the era of apartheid and provocatively sat in the wrong place on a bus. When he was told to move, he asked why. 'Because you are white.' 'No, I am not,' McCabe answered, 'I'm Irish.'

One of my favourite nuggets from Fr Herbert McCabe is, 'We are not just human beings, but human becomings ...'

Fr Radcliffe quotes Zygmunt Bauman. 'We live in what we now call a liquid modernity. It is a world of short-term commitments whether at work, at home or in ones religion. The average American has eleven jobs in a lifetime ... divorces are frequent. People drift from one religion to another, like bees getting nectar. But being baptised is not like enrolling in a gym with temporary membership. As is tattooed on the flank of the actor Megan Fox of the film *Transformers*: 'those who danced were thought to be quite insane by those who could not hear the music.'

Apropos of nothing Fr Radcliffe tells us that Margaret Thatcher's nickname was TINA: There Is No Alternative. I love that.

I like his version of a story which is often attributed to St Philip Neri, but in Radcliffe's book becomes a famous 'Rabbi story'. Either way it gives us pause for thought. 'The story is told of a Rabbi who is driven mad by a woman in the Synagogue who was always gossiping about everyone, spreading nasty stories. And so one day he took her to the top of a high tower and asked her to empty the contents of a pillow. The feathers drifted all over town. Then he said; 'Now go and collect all the feathers.' She replied, 'Rabbi this isn't possible; they are everywhere.' And he said, 'It is the same with your nasty words.' And so it is.

BREATHING UNDER WATER

23 October 2011

'The addiction to our own way of thinking is probably the greatest addiction we have. We are often not aware of our own addictions.' That quotation stopped me in my tracks. The more I think about it, the more uncomfortable I become. And the more uncomfortable I become, the more truth I see in the statement.

It comes from Fr Richard Rohr, the well-known Franciscan writer. In his book about the spirituality of The Twelve Steps of AA, *Breathing Under Water*, Rohr tries to help struggling people to come to terms with their own brokenness and to experience healing. Rohr makes the case that the Twelve Step Programme of Alcoholics Anonymous is rooted in Christian teaching; so much so, that on a practical level, it continues the healing mission of Jesus to today's world. The Twelve Step Programme and the gospel interrelate because of the way they lead to forgiveness and healing.

Rohr believes that we are all addicts in one way or another. Individuals are addicts but so too are institutions, nations and cultures. Each has its own form of neurosis.

He believes that our contemporary Western culture focuses on greed, money, sensual desires and the importance of being in control.

America is addicted to oil, war and power. The church, among other things, has become addicted to its own self-importance.

Unearthing gospel principles in the Twelve-Step Programme, he discovered, 'how helpful it is to view sin like addiction, as a disease, a very destructive disease, instead of merely something that was culpable, punishable, or that made God unhappy. If sin indeed did make God unhappy, it is because God desires nothing more than our happiness, and the healing of our disease.' Obviously healing was always at the centre of Jesus' ministry.

Part of the spirituality of Richard Rohr is that he is more concerned about healing in the here and now than he is about some mysterious reward in the afterlife.

Rohr accuses Christianity of concentrating on dogmas rather than on practical steps to human fulfilment. His theory is that great damage was done when Christianity became the official religion of the Roman Empire. It was at that point, Rohr says, 'that Christianity began to place theory over practice. Christians began to ritualise worship of Jesus, instead of following Jesus in practical ways.'

The great insight of the Twelve Steps is the acceptance of our own powerlessness. That is a fundamental starting point. As Rohr discovers, 'powerlessness is the place where Jesus touched those he met most deeply,' according to the gospels.

A major problem for all who suffer blind addiction is denial. As Jesus put it, 'We see the splinter in our brother or sister's eye and miss the log in our own.'

Real spirituality depends on us recognising that we are totally dependent on God for everything and that of ourselves we are powerless.

'Alcoholics have their powerlessness visible for all to see. The rest of us disguise it in different ways and overcompensate for our more hidden addictions and attachments, especially our addiction to our own way of thinking ... we keep doing the same thing over and over again, even if it is not working for us,' Rohr writes.

I was taken aback when Rohr wrote, 'I now have more people telling me they are "recovering Catholics" than those in recovery from addiction ... perhaps we failed to give them the good news they desired, needed, and expected?'

And here's another breathtaking insight from Rohr, 'Unless religion moves people to the mystical it becomes more a problem than it is a solution.' Such food for the soul is rare in modern spiritual direction.

Finally Rohr says that the paradox of both the Twelve-Step Programme and the gospel teaching is that in surrendering one wins; in giving one keeps, and in dying, one comes to life.

REMBRANT AND ME

10 July 2011

The first time I saw a reproduction of Rembrandt's, *The Return Of The Prodigal Son* I wept. In front of me was the most moving explanation of the gospel story of the prodigal son I had ever encountered and I really understood the meaning of the gospel story for the first time. What made me weep was the realisation that I don't have to be perfect to be loved by God. It was Rembrandt's genius which broke open my heart.

Rembrandt painted *The Return Of The Prodigal Son* towards the end of his life. Repeated personal tragedy, and his own wayward life, fractured his relationship with God. But he experienced reconciliation as he worked on this 'spiritual' masterpiece.

The gospel account has the patient father welcoming home a wayward son, whilst at the same time, placating an elder son who never did anything wrong.

I'm told Rembrandt worked hard to find a friendly, compassionate face for the father, who is meant to embody God's forgiveness for all our sins. In the painting the prodigal son's shaved head is buried deep in the father's breast. It is the body of a carefree young man, yet at the same time, the 'head' of an infant on a journey to rebirth from the father's bosom.

This prodigal son is dressed in a pilgrim's outer garment. His left foot has no sandal and this bare foot highlights that he is a penitent in need of forgiveness. The right foot, with its well-worn sandal, tells us this is a pilgrim with many miles still to travel. The conclusion is that reconciliation is both the end of a journey and the beginning of a new life.

However the hands of the father are the most striking. Those familiar with Rembrandt's paintings recognise both hands from previous works. The father's left hand is placed on the shoulder of the returning prodigal son. It's a strong supportive hand; a trusting hand – a man's hand.

Amazingly, the father's right hand is completely different. This is a woman's hand. In Rembrandt's other works this woman's hand recalls a caring, forgiving, loving person. Just as the feet represent both penance and pilgrimage, so the father's hands represent strength and gentleness.

The saddest person in the painting and in the story is the elder son who looks on from the outside. In his own mind he never made a mistake so he doesn't know the need for forgiveness. His self-righteousness imprisons him in his begrudgery.

When I first studied the painting I arrogantly saw myself as the prodigal son. In a sense I am. Yet I am also the elder son, the begrudger, the self-righteous one. What I need to become however is a person who is more like the father. I need to learn the father's gentleness, strength, love, forgiveness and wisdom.

This painting taught me that for a prodigal son to return, he first has to admit his mistakes. I now know that all of my inner speeches of justification for my life are but repetitions of the prodigal son's, 'I will go to my father and say ...'

I've learned that the father has to love both the prodigal son and the begrudging elder son equally. Most of all Rembrandt's two beautiful hands – the masculine and the feminine – assure me that God is both a father and a mother – the perfect parent.

This painting made me realise that I can never earn God's forgiveness; I simply must be humble enough to accept it. That's why I wept when I first saw it.

THE NOTHING PEOPLE

8 January 2012

About a year ago I gave a lift to a man outside Athy. He was thumbing back home and he told me that he lived twenty miles from where he was thumbing. I was able to bring him the whole way and we had a chat as we travelled along. He had a problem with drink. That's what he admitted to. It was obvious that he was a raving alcoholic, but no alcoholic ever has anything more than a 'little problem with drink'.

A couple of days previously his family had gathered him into the back of a car and sent him to Sr Consilio's place in Athy. What they expected her to do I'm not quite sure. He was first washed and then brought to the opening lecture.

At the opening lecture, he told me, he was put off: 'Do you know what they asked me to do? They wanted me to change my whole life. And when I heard that I got out of it as soon as I could.'

Isn't that a tragedy? He got a chance to change his life. He got a chance to be rescued from the demon that was destroying him. But in his own mind the road which was pointed out to him, which would lead to life, seemed impossible to travel.

Little did he know that the road he actually took was even more impossible. It certainly was a dead end. Because unless he changes his whole life, he will die, if he's not dead already.

It is easy to identify that choice in another's life. The same opportunity is given to us through baptism, through the Eucharist, through the sacraments, through our Christian life. And just as frequently, we decide to stay on the road we are on, and to die sad but undisturbed. We have the choice to change and grow and live and suffer and reach new life or to avoid trouble, remain the same and fizzle out long before we are dead.

That's a definition of a nothing person. And maybe I should finish with *The Nothing People*.

They do not lie;
    they just neglect to tell the truth.
They do not take;
    they simply cannot bring themselves to give.
They do not steal;
    they scavenge.
They will not rock the boat;
    but did you ever see them pull an oar!
They will not pull you down;
    they'll simply let you pull them up
    and let that pull you down.
They do not hurt you;
    they merely will not help you.
They do not hate you;
    they merely cannot love you.
They do not burn you;
    they just fiddle while you burn.
They are the nothing people:
    the sins of omission people.
    the neither-good-nor-bad
    and therefore worse.
Because the good at least keep busy trying.
    and the bad try just as hard.
Both have that character
    that comes from caring, action and conviction.
So give me every time
    an honest sinner, or even a saint.
But, God and Satan get together
    and protect me from the nothing people.

                                          Anonymous

THE LONELY EMBER

7 August 2011

A member of a church, who previously had been attending services regularly, stopped going. After a few weeks, the priest decided to visit him. It was a chilly evening.

The priest found the man at home alone, sitting before a blazing fire. Guessing the reason for his priest's visit, the man welcomed him, led him to a big chair near the fireplace and waited. The priest made himself comfortable but said nothing. In silence, he contemplated the flames of the burning logs.

After a while the priest took the fire tongs, carefully picked up a brightly burning ember and placed it to one side of the hearth on its own. Then he sat back in his chair, still silent. The host was fascinated.

As the one lone ember's flame diminished, there was a momentary glow and then its fire was no more.

Just before the priest was ready to leave, he picked up the cold, dead ember and placed it back in the middle of the fire. Immediately it began to glow once more with the light and warmth of the burning logs around it. As the priest reached the door to leave, his host said, 'Thank you so much for your visit and especially for the fiery sermon. I shall be back in church next Sunday.'

RABINDRANATH TAGORE

1 July 2012

Because of the manner in which the bits and pieces of life fall together, I've spent these past few months reflecting on the 'journey' of my life wondering where the years spent in priesthood and religious life have led me.

That in turn brought me back to the saintly Thomas Merton. Discernment for him meant discarding layers of pious practices rather than being swamped by useless devotion. I've read about and reflected on the efficacy of passive resistance pioneered by Mahatma Gandhi. In the process and almost by accident I rediscovered the writings of Rabindranath Tagore.

It's ever more obvious that this twenty-first century will be dominated by the cultures of China and India. The economies of the world will be rescued by the massive populations of both India and China. It was in that context that Tagore took on a new importance for me.

He was born one hundred and fifty years ago and died in 1941. During his eighty years on this earth he became one of India's best known poets. In the East a poet does more than write verse. Typically Tagore's greatest contributions were in education, religion, sociology and politics.

As a Hindu, Tagore valued all religious traditions and longed for people to experience the wonders of the human spirit itself. For someone who came through the Caste system in India, this openness proved shocking to his contemporaries.

Tagore preached the universal message of divine love which, of necessity embraces people of all faiths and backgrounds. He attempted to overcome barriers which individual faiths set up between people.

Tagore was equally broad-minded when it came to politics. He detested a nationalism which lead to the separation of people. He believed that our first loyalty should be to humanity itself.

'Pride and patriotism is not for me, I earnestly hope that I should find my home anywhere in the world before I leave it,' he once wrote.

He identified with people who suffered, especially those who had to endure death and loss in their family. His mother died while he was still a boy and a short time later his sister-in-law died by suicide. When he himself was forty-one his wife died, followed closely by the deaths of three of their children under the age of ten. That's why his poems and writings keep searching for a love which can be found only in darkness.

Gandhi and Tagore were contemporaries who both loved their native people but who rarely agreed on the basic principles of how India's freedom could be achieved. They were both deeply religious men, but Tagore disagreed with Gandhi's principle of passive resistance. Tagore said that passive resistance was not necessarily a moral choice, because it can be used against truth as well as for it.

It was many decades before his writings were appreciated in the West, mainly because his English is remarkably quaint and sounds as if it has been taken directly from the King James Bible. However he was named the first non-European Nobel Prize Winner for Literature in 1913.

Tagore lived through World War I and the beginning of World War II yet never lost faith in humanity. 'As I look around I see the crumbling ruins of a proud civilisation strewn like a vast heap of futility. And yet I shall not commit the grievous sin of losing faith in Man ... I would rather look forward to the opening of a new chapter in its history.'

His poem *Closed Path* has awakened my interest in Tagore.

> *I thought that my voyage had come to its end*
> *at the last limit of my power – that the path before me was*
>   *closed,*
> *that provisions were exhausted*
> *and the time come to take shelter in a silent obscurity.*
>
> *But I find that thy will knows no end in me.*
> *And when old words die on the tongue,*
> *new melodies break forth from the heart;*
> *and where the old tracks are lost,*
> *new country is revealed with its wonders.*

What a wonderful description of the journey of life!

SECOND FIDDLE

24 June 2012

The church must regard the feast of John the Baptist as important since it is one of those rare occasions when a feast day displaces the proper Sunday.

The name John means 'the Lord is gracious' and that is important. John's name reminds us that the Lord is indeed gracious.

It is interesting that the birth of John the Baptist comes at what should be the brightest time of the year, on 24 June. The birth of his cousin Jesus is celebrated at what is the darkest time of the year, 25 December, close to the winter solstice. John is one who comes to prepare a way for the Lord.

The American conductor Leonard Bernstein was once asked to explain the most difficult instrument in the Orchestra to play. He replied, 'The second fiddle. I can get plenty of first violinists, but to get someone who can play second fiddle with enthusiasm, that's a problem. And if we have no second fiddle we have no harmony.'

In the Bible the best example of second fiddle is John the Baptist. He was willing to move aside when Jesus came. He was willing to let another step into the limelight.

There aren't many other examples of enthusiastic second fiddles in church life.

TAKING LIFE EASY

10 July 2011

We must be the luckiest people in the world, living here in Ireland. Times are hard but life itself doesn't have to be. It's summer; it's holiday time. So grab the opportunity to do the things you want to – instead of things you have to. Remember the Talmud's wisdom: 'We will have to answer to God for the permissible pleasures that we failed to enjoy.'

I'm the world's worst person to give advice about taking life easy because I'm perpetual motion personified. But even I realise there comes a time when I can do nothing better than to do nothing.

At this point in my life I get edgy doing nothing because I've deceived myself into believing that my worth is in my work. Nonsense. Who I am is what counts – not what I do.

Where I live, Lough Erne, is a huge mass of water which has hundreds of little islands dotted around it. My favourite way to do nothing is to lose myself on one of those lonely islands.

At first the silence teases me. Then it threatens me. Just when it is almost unbearable, silence breaks open my soul and I listen. I listen to the fish jumping for joy in the still waters; I listen to vulnerable birds whistling their healing tunes from atop the leafy trees; I listen to the holy breezes gently breathing new life into the blossoming flowers; I listen to the rustling bushes and the whispering fields of tall grass.

When I do nothing I become aware of the simple pleasures; I'm happy just to be. It's then I'm overcome with gratitude. Gratitude turns what we have into enough, chaos into order, a stranger into a friend, a meal into a feast and a house into a home. As author Melody Beattie put it: 'Gratitude makes sense of our past, brings peace for today, and creates a vision for tomorrow.'

The greatest gift you can give yourself costs nothing; you don't have to go anywhere; you don't have to do anything. Just do nothing. Your only obligation is to be true to yourself.

Take time to reflect and appreciate your own goodness. That's the spirit of happiness. It was Napoleon who wisely said: 'Only those who live in the spirit can bring about change, the rest of us merely rearrange things.'

HARD WORDS FOR PREACHERS

8 July 2012

I came across the following words from the Jewish theologian and preacher Rabbi Abraham Joshua Heschel. We priests need to keep these words in front of us as we write our homily each week.

'Religion declines not because it was refuted, but because it became irrelevant, dull, oppressive, insipid. When faith is completely replaced by creed, worship by discipline, love by habit; when the crisis of today is ignored because of the splendor of the past; when faith becomes an heirloom rather than a living fountain; when religion speaks only in the name of authority rather than the voice of compassion, its message becomes meaningless.'

HAPPINESS

May 2012

Years ago I studied in Chicago. The author John Powell gave us a talk called 'Happiness Is An Inside Job.' He said when life is tough we can still be happy because happiness is an inside job. God wants us to be happy both in this world and in the next.

So here are my 'Top Tips' for happiness:

1. We must accept ourselves as we are. I am who I am and all the wishing in the world won't change me. Just play the hand your dealt.

2. There is no point blaming others for the choices I make. I have to accept responsibility for my life and the choices I make.

3. Choose a balanced life. Work, relax, exercise, eat properly. Have fun too!

4. Learn to love what you have to do. Help others out of love and not because you have to.

5. Challenge is a necessary part of life. Don't get stuck in a rut. Be brave and move out of the comfort zones.

6. See the positive instead of the negative. Make life a discovery of what is good.

7. Stop trying to be perfect. The perfect is the enemy of the good. Wanting to be prefect will destroy you.

8. Powell added that being able to express yourself well is an important part of happiness. Effective communication of how you feel – your doubts, your feelings, your hopes and desires – helps others to understand you.

9. Have a Higher Power, and spend time reflecting with that higher power.

I remember thinking then, as I do now, that this is all plain common sense. I believe most of us are happier than we realise. So don't be guilty; 'Don't worry – be happy.'

EASTER SUNDAY

4 April 2010

It is such a hard time to be full of joy and hope. We have the scandals in the church. We have the Ryan Report, the Murphy Report and the Magdalene Laundries Report. We just wonder what is happening to our church and not only that but to our society itself. We have the economy, unemployment, Haiti and we have the huge difficulty in the Quinn Group. It just seems to me it is hard to see the glory for the gloom. And the quotation from the gospel which comes to mind is 'Jesus wept' rather than 'Jesus is risen.'

And yet Easter reminds us that there is hope, that people are good, that faith is still there and that faith is personal and nobody can take our faith away from us. It's a reminder that, as Archbishop Tutu recently said, 'Every act of kindness enhances the quality of life.'

- Easter says there is hope despite the fear and despair.

- Easter says that love is pulling us out of our own tombs of despair.

- Easter helps us to recognise the love of God in the hug of one who cares for us.

Somebody recently asked me a very good question. 'Is there anyone left we can trust?' And that's the problem. We seem to have run out of leaders in every part of our life and we are left in a very sad place.

On Friday night we had a most wonderful example of a Passion mime. It spoke louder than any words could ever do. It was the perfect example of actions speaking louder than words. And yet we also have the experience of Easter. It gives us a sense of hope and joy inside that it is hard to put words on. We know words fail us when we try to express it but we know also that the experience is real.

Words fail us at first when the Word of God redeems us.

We know that our church is a mess. But look at the church in the gospel today. The disciples were disillusioned. The one they loved, the one they put their trust in, the one they presumed was their saviour. The one they believed was their Messiah, was put to death as a mere criminal and stuffed in a tomb with stones rolled over it so that he would never be heard of again. It's a terrible ending for a leader that you have put your trust in. So the disciples knew what it was like to be absolutely leaderless. The gospel today indicates that they are running around like headless chickens. Have you ever heard so many people rushing. Mary rushes to the tomb because she wants to be alone. She wasn't expecting resurrection. She was expecting a dead body and was very disappointed when she didn't find it.

Then she ran back and said somebody has taken the body. She gets John and Peter to run the whole way back to the tomb. John wins the race, but he's young and he's afraid of dead bodies so he doesn't go to look because he was expecting a dead body. Peter comes, out of breath and last, but he goes in because he is experienced. When he doesn't find a dead body he comes back out saying that the cloths belong to Jesus but the body is not there. It is John then who is the first to believe.

Out of it all they realised that Jesus is risen from the dead and that their failure, defeat, depression and lack of faith is gone forever. They know that no matter what happens, Jesus is now alive and that it's a whole new church and a whole new experience for them.

We can learn from them. Each of us knows deep down that we have faith. That's why you are here. You believe, even though you can't put words on it, that Jesus is risen from the dead; it means so much to you and to the community. The church as we experience it may well die. But we know that faith will never die as long as each of us believes.

Our faith is a gift from God and nobody can take it from us. It is ours. For many years I have been trying to preach and talk about what the Second Vatican Council called 'the People Of God'. That's where the church is. But I felt no one believed me. And I know you didn't believe it either because you thought the church belonged to the priests, bishops and pope. Now we know it doesn't. And that's a wonderful sign of hope. This is a new direction. And it's a good time to be alive. We know that there is a new church on the way, but we are not sure what that church will look like.

Listen to the prayer in today's Mass … 'Let our celebration today raise us up and renew our lives by the Spirit ….' Look what is told to us in the Exsultet: 'This is the night that dispels all evil … the night that brings mourners joy … the night when heaven is wedded to earth and when we are reconciled with God.' What more assurance or reassurance could we want.

We are beginning to experience in our lives a new way of church and that will help us to create a new church. Don't wait for somebody to solve your problems for you. Live it and the problems will solve themselves. That's where the joy, the hope and the love come from.

Easter reminds us to roll away the stones and rocks that seal our hopes and dreams in the tombs of despair and cynicism.

It reminds me of a story about a man whom I tried to help in his final illness. He was dying slowly from cancer in hospital. He was finding it hard to die. One day I listened to him quietly and must have said something to him because shortly afterwards a letter arrived in the post from him in which he told me that he was beginning to feel graced at this time in his life. In fact he thought that now was the most graced part of his life. The love and the care and the peace which he got from those looking after him showed that God still cares. And then he wrote: 'Thanks for helping me to choose life in this time of fear and uncertainty. "Something wondrous is afoot." I just can't see it yet.' Isn't that a magnificent and beautiful thing. 'Something wondrous is afoot.' That's what's wonderful in our lives and that's what Easter promises. 'Something wondrous is afoot.' We might not be able to see it yet. It is what made St Paul write so optimistically from behind prison walls to the Philippians (4:4): 'Rejoice in the Lord always. Again I say rejoice.' It's why Jesus could say just after his last meal with his friends (John 15), 'I am saying these things to you that my joy may be in you and that your joy may be complete.'

REFLECTION: ONE

One song can spark a moment,
One flower can wake a dream,
One tree can start a forest,
One bird can herald spring,
One smile begins a friendship,
One handclasp lifts a soul,
One star can guide a ship at sea,
One vote can change a nation,
One sunbeam lights a room,
One candle wipes out darkness,
One laugh will lift sadness,
One step must start each journey,
One word must start each prayer,
One hope will raise our spirits,
One touch can show you care,
One voice can speak with wisdom,
One heart can know what's true,
One life can make the difference,
You see it's up to you!

Author Unknown

FEAR AND HOPE

20 May 2012

The feast of the Ascension makes me sad. Maybe it's that picture of the disciples looking up to heaven and seeing the one they loved disappearing behind the clouds. They were given the task of carrying on but they didn't feel equipped for it. The one they depended on was gone. It's up to them now.

It was only recently that I became aware again that in the early days of the church they celebrated the Resurrection, Ascension and Pentecost as one feast. Jesus rising from the dead, going to heaven and the Holy Spirit coming down upon those who were left behind was one feast celebrated on the same day. Taken as one single mystery it makes more sense.

St Teresa of Avila's famous prayer tells us what our vocation is now. 'Christ has no body but yours now on earth; no hands but yours; no feet but yours; yours are the eyes through which Christ's compassion looks out on the world; yours are the feet with which he is to go about doing good; yours are the hands with which he is to bless us now.' We are to be the compassion, the mercy and the gentleness of God to those in most of need of all three.

The Ascension means that Jesus is gone to heaven, not to distance himself from us but to prepare a place for us at the right hand of God. That too is an inspiring image. We are loved by God and we can hope to be with God at the end of life. What prevents us from acting out what Jesus has tasked us with?

The great novelist Iris Murdoch wrestled with all the themes of love and fear. And she once wrote, 'If you want to understand another person, ask of what they are afraid.'

When I first read that I thought about it for a long time and then I realised it is a question to be put to myself. If you want to understand me, ask of what I am afraid.

Our fears dominate us. It is of course our love that should dominate us.

It has been said, 'Love is the love of being in love.' That's explained in a threefold way.

1. We fall in love which is the exciting part.
2. We learn to love which is the hard part.
3. We love being loving which is the best part.

When loving others becomes the centre of our lives then we experience the peace that love brings.

I heard Fr Peter McVerry speaking recently. He told us he entered the Jesuits because he was educated there and his family were professional people and that the Jesuits seemed the most natural place for him. Early in his career he decided he wanted to work with the homeless in Dublin. That changed his relationship with God and his way of being a religious and a priest. He tried to explain how much he had learned from being homeless. In fact he learned that the basis of our relationship with God is to be constantly homeless.

On one occasion a young boy, not yet a teenager was brought into his home by the authorities. It seemed that those who were caring for him disappeared. He was on the streets, was rescued and brought into Peter's house for homeless people. He stayed with Peter and got some sort of schooling whilst he was there.

At the age of eighteen he met a girl and wanted to do what every normal person would want, i.e. set up a home. So he left the hostel and went to live with his girlfriend. Things seemed to go well for a little while but as can often happen with eighteen-year-olds after about a year their relationship broke up and the girl left. Once again he was homeless.

But this time he hadn't the heart to start over again so he went to the canal and jumped in trying to drown himself. Much to his disgust he was saved and brought to a hospital where Peter went to see him. During their conversation the young man asked Peter, 'Do you know what's the worst thing about being homeless?

Peter thought for a while and gave the obvious answer. The worst thing about being homeless was having nowhere to call home. Nowhere to go at night. No address, no identity. The boy said that was difficult but it was not the worst thing.

Peter then thought perhaps being hungry all the time must be one of the worst things about being homeless. The young man agreed that hunger, without knowing where your next bite to eat will come from, is a terrible place to be. But after a while you learn to stretch the little scraps you get and steal enough to make sure that the cold edge of hunger doesn't overcome you.

Peter then wondered was it boredom with nowhere to go and nothing to do all day.

The young man said it was bad but you got used to it. He then offered the solution. The worst thing about being homeless is that you can't go on living knowing that nobody cares whether you live or die. That's what spiritual and emotional homelessness means.

It is worth thinking about that when Jesus preached his message of hope, people listened to him all day. No sermon was too long, they even forgot that they were hungry. At the end of the day it was Jesus who said that they needed something to eat. The people seemed to be in some sort of mystical state that they experienced neither tiredness nor hunger.

So what was it that Jesus was preaching that attracted the crowds, and made them forget everything. Whatever it was they found the message of Jesus to be life-giving. Since we are Jesus on earth today, for the people, we should do the same. Yet nobody trusts, nobody believes and few care about what the church says.

In the time of Jesus the religious people concentrated on rules and regulations and structures. Jesus preached something that was more life-giving. He preached the compassionate face of God and his preaching gave them life. Jesus was the compassion of God and God's passion is compassion.

Look at the second reading, 'Bear with one another charitably. Have complete selflessness, gentleness and patience. Preserve the unity of the Spirit by the peace that binds you together. There is one Lord, one faith, one baptism and one God who is father of all … we all have different gifts, apostles, evangelists, pastors, teachers, so that together we build up the Body of Christ.

God has promised to love us unconditionally from the moment of conception for all eternity. No matter what we do or don't do God never stops loving us. We may not love God. Everything, and especially the Eucharist, is in thanksgiving for the eternal love God gives us. It's not built on commandments or obligations. It's based on love and gratitude. That's how we make the compassionate face of God present.

The most important idea of all is that we must have hope. And hope means that we must be people of hope ourselves. We must keep on going, keep on doing what is right. Keep on loving, keep on being the face of God's compassion and mercy and gentleness.

St Augustine said, 'Hope has two beautiful daughters. Anger and courage. Anger at the way things are; courage to see that they do not remain the same forever.'

That to me is an acceptable way to proceed. That's the vocation of a Christian on this Ascension Day.

To Live is to Risk

2 January 2011

To laugh is to risk appearing the fool.
To weep is to risk appearing sentimental.
To reach out for another is to risk involvement.
To expose feelings is to risk exposing your true self.
To place your ideas, your dreams, before the crowd is to
risk their loss.
To love is to risk not being loved in return.
To live is to risk dying.
To hope is to risk despair.
To try at all is to risk failure.
But risk we must. Because the greatest hazard to life is
to risk nothing.
The person who risks nothing has nothing, does nothing, is
*   nothing –*
They may avoid suffering and sorrow, but they simply
cannot learn, feel, change, grow, love, live.
Chained by their certitudes they are slaves; they have
forfeited freedom.
Only the person who risks can be called free – and
only someone who is free can be called a child of God.

Isn't it strange?

15 May 2011

Isn't it strange how a £20 note seems like such a large amount when you donate it to church, but such a small amount when you go shopping?

Isn't it strange how two hours seem so long when you're at church, and how short they seem when you're watching a good movie?

Isn't it strange that you can't find a word to say when you're praying, but you have no trouble thinking what to talk about with a friend?

Isn't it strange how difficult and boring it is to read one chapter of the Bible but how easy it is to read one hundred pages of a popular novel?

Isn't it strange how everyone wants front-row tickets to concerts or games but they do whatever is possible to sit in the last row in church?

Isn't it strange how we need to know about an event for church two to three weeks before the day so we can include it in our agenda, but we can adjust it for other events at the last minute?

Isn't it strange how difficult it is to learn a fact about God to share it with others but how easy it is to learn, understand, extend and repeat gossip?

Isn't it strange how we believe everything that magazines and newspapers say but we question the words in the Bible?

CHRISTMAS HYMNS AND CAROLS

25 December 2011

Hymn singing in church is an essential part of worship and was originally modelled on the Book of Psalms. Hymns are easily memorised, contain solid doctrine for that Christian religious group, and in an age before printing, hymn singing helped to commit to memory the essential doctrines of faith.

Eventually they wrote hymns for seasonal themes in the church's year. There are hymns for Lent, Easter, Advent and Christmas. At first many hymns were dull and sombre, but then the art of writing Christmas carols became popular. Inevitably these were joyous songs retelling the Nativity story. St Francis of Assisi is credited with introducing carols to church services in the thirteenth century.

Many of the carols have their own unusual history. None more so than *Silent Night*.

Silent Night was first performed on 24 December 1818 at St Nicholas in Oberndorf in Austria. Fr Joseph Mohr wrote the lyrics a few years earlier and asked Franz Gruber a musician, to compose a melody for his Christmas Eve Mass in 1818.

There are many other disputed legends about the writing of the carol. The most famous is that the organ in the church was out of order because a mouse had eaten through the bellows. According to the story Fr Mohr had problems due to his drinking, and allowed the church organ go into disrepair. As a result, Gruber had to compose *Stille Nacht, Heilege Nacht* to be preformed with the guitar.

In any case *Silent Night* is a simple melody. That's not the case with Handel's *Messiah*. This is always performed by well-rehearsed choral groups during Advent. It was first presented in Dublin during Lent in 1742.

The composer of *God Rest Ye Merry Gentlemen* is unknown but the lyrics are reputed to go back to the fifteenth century. Charles Dickens portrays Ebenezer Scrooge becoming upset when he hears this cheerful tune being sung.

Away In A Manger is another classic with many myths attached to it. It was first published in 1885 in a Lutheran Sunday School book, and this creates a misconception that Martin Luther wrote the lyrics. Many sources still credit Luther with its authorship but experts agree the author is unknown.

The Good King Wenceslas commemorates a Catholic bohemian martyr who becomes famous for giving alms to the poor. John Mason Neale published the song in 1853 and is credited with translating the words. The melody is Finnish and was composed hundreds of years earlier. What is unusual about the good king is that there is no mention of the Nativity at all. It becomes a Christmas carol because of its reference to St Stephen whose feast day is the day after Christmas.

Isaac Watts wrote the lyrics of *Joy To The World* and the English clergyman is credited with writing over six hundred hymns. The melody is often attributed to Handel though we now know it to be the work of American Lowell Mason.

Charles Wesley wrote *Hark The Herald Angels Sing*, but when he wrote it, it was *Hark Hear The Welkin Ring*. The Welkin referred to the skies and the heavens. The words have been tweaked down through the centuries to its present format. Felix Mendelssohn wrote the melody to commemorate Gutenberg's invention of the printing press.

My favourite carol is *O Holy Night* and it originated as a poem by Placide Cappeau. He was a French wine merchant and poet who answered a request from his Parish Priest to write a poem for Christmas. Placide asked his friend Aldophe Adam to write the music. It was translated into English by John Dwight. Initially church authorities frowned upon *O Holy Night*; one French bishop went so far as to denounce it for its lack of musical taste and total absence of the spirit of religion. Maybe that's why I like it so much.

A lesser known carol is *Let There Be Peace On Earth*. It was inspired by Gill Jackson's struggle with depression during World War II. She was a single mother who became so depressed that she attempted to take her own life. In a search for peace she found Christianity. Then during the Korean War in the 1950s she was praying for an end to the conflict when she wrote the words, 'Let There Be Peace On Earth'. Later her husband, songwriter Sy Miller, wrote the melody.

So fill your home with carols over the Christmas period – they are inspiring, nostalgic and help us to have a spirit-filled, joyous Christmas.

CHRISTMAS CUSTOMS AND TRADITIONS

23 December 2012

Every country has its own customs for Christmas and Ireland is no exception. When I was growing up, we never ate meat on St Stephen's Day. Even though the goose was left over from Christmas Day and there were no fridges to store it in, my mother insisted that all of us abstain from meat. We didn't question her much and we all did it because it was supposed to bring the gift of good health in the coming year. I don't know the origin of the practice and I don't know any other family who did it. So maybe my mother made up her own customs.

The Christmas season is full of interesting facts. Every year seems to throw up more of them. Only this year I discovered the word mistletoe means, 'dung-on-a-twig'. Apparently it's an Anglo-Saxon word and that is its literal meaning. The custom of kissing under the mistletoe is just as unusual. It comes from the ancient druids of Ireland. It was their belief that whenever enemies met under the mistletoe in a forest, they had to lay down their arms and observe a truce until the next day. I suppose it was a kiss and make-up custom.

Here's a piece of information which is not a theory, it's a fact. In Ireland alone the wrapping paper from our presents over the Christmas period is equivalent to the weight of four thousand elephants. Add to that wine bottles, cans, chocolate boxes and the experts estimate that there will be one hundred and thirty million containers of rubbish sent to landfills sites in the New Year. What a load of rubbish that is!

Another fact is that the Samaritans, throughout the country, will get a call every seven seconds over the Christmas period. People given to depression and loneliness are at greater danger during the Christmas period when everybody else seems to be enjoying the fun. If you need to talk at any time during the year be sure to call the Samaritans, where you can talk anonymously and confidentially twenty-four hours a day.

Another unpalatable fact is that these December days are the most dangerous on Irish roads. It's probably because so many people are making last minute dashes and others are prepared to take the risk of a drink too many. The young are mainly to blame because forty per cent of insurance claims for fatal accidents involve people under the age of twenty-nine. The motto must be *don't drink and drive*, and don't get into a car with anyone who is drinking and driving. It's just not worth it.

Another surprising fact that I discovered this week was that Santa is able to speak two thousand seven hundred languages. At least he needs to because that's the number of languages in the world and there are seven thousand dialects. We know Santa speaks every single one of them. What a brain!

And finally to those who want to take Christ out of Christmas, let me remind you that in 1647 Christmas was actually banned in England. Under Oliver Cromwell anyone caught celebrating Christmas was arrested on the spot. The ban lasted for thirteen years. Needless to say it didn't work and those who want to take Christ out of Christmas would do well to remember that.

RESPECT, LOVE, JOY AND PEACE

30 December 2012

In the prayer today there is a nice summary of the characteristics that people living together should have. 'May we be united in respect and love ... Bring us to the joy and peace of your eternal home.' So there you have it. Respect, love, joy and peace. Let's take each of them one by one.

Respect

In life I would like respect not for what I do, or what I am. I don't really want respect because I am a priest. I would much rather have respect because I am a human being and I like to be respected for what I try to be because it doesn't matter whether I succeed or fail.

Love

Love is a word we don't like using these days. Somebody described a family as F.A.M.I.L.Y. which equals Father And Mother I Love You. It means that we appreciate the efforts of others. That we speak well of others. For example in today's second reading we have a wonderful phrase which summaries a Christian: 'Believe in the name of his Son Jesus Christ and love one another.' That's a wonderful definition of a good family. Good families are sometimes holy and sometimes not. God can deal with that.

Joy

Joy is hard to define, but is your home one of joy or is it one of fear. Are people happy to come to your home? Is there a tension, either spoken or unspoken? Is your house known for praising people or for running them down? Does it make little of people or does it encourage people? Does it bring out the best in people? A good description of a joyful home is where people are encouraged to be the best they can be.

Peace

This is a difficult one to define as well. Am I easy to live with or do I rule by silences and bullying? There used to be a phrase around our country about a man who was nice to the neighbours but not his own family. They'd say he was a person who hung his fiddle outside his door. It was the same as saying he was a street angel and a house devil.

Am I contrary? Do I bully? Do I always want my own way? Do I keep control and are people able to relax in our home. They are very ordinary virtues.

If you look at the Holy Family it wasn't that perfect. That's the first thing we must realise: that there is not and there never has been, any such thing as a perfect family. There are people who try and sometimes fail.

Joseph was a widower. He had doubts about how Mary got pregnant. He was looking for a handy way out. But eventually he was told in prayer that it would all work out. So he stuck with it and that's the fact that made him good.

Mary was a teenager who could have been stoned to death for the condition she was in. She was full of fear and had to be told numerous times by the angel not to be afraid.

Jesus himself was an outcast and a failure. And as you can see in today's gospel they also had their arguments. How many mothers have repeated Mary's words in the gospel today. 'Son why have you done this to us?'

There will be many times when we are lost.

You try your best; you look after your family; you get too busy doing good; you lose Jesus from your life. Things go wrong; relationships break up; you feel a failure; you suffer a grief too much. You lose Jesus. God doesn't hear your prayers; you lose Jesus. The church angers you and its leaders are out of touch, so you react by staying away – you lose the precious gift of faith.

The reality is that even when we lose Jesus, Jesus is not lost to us. If we look we will find him. We will find our true selves in the middle of our lost state. Keep searching and keep pondering.

One last little tip which I will pass on to you. Secrecy is the enemy of good relationships. Families which pretend to be something they are not, are unhealthy families. Accept that the family I come from is as it is and do the best I can; get on with it!

Try to encourage respect, love, joy and peace. It's easier said than done but at least it's practical.

LEO TOLSTOY'S STORY

30 December 2012

One of my favourite stories is Leo Tolstoy's Russian tale, which I'll paraphrase for you until you're lucky enough to read it in full yourself.

In a little Russian town there lived a cobbler, Martin. He lived in a tiny basement with one window, which looked onto the street above. From the front window he could see only feet passing by. But that was all he needed to see. He recognised people by their shoes, since he had made most of them.

He was a good man, and in old age when his wife died, he spent the longer winter nights reading his Bible by candlelight. One night he read about a man who invited Jesus into his house and didn't even offer water to wash his feet. Yet a sinful woman, an outcast, anointed his feet.

Martin thought long and hard how he would welcome Jesus, should he ever come to visit him. Martin feared he might be like the man who didn't welcome Jesus properly.

He drifted off to sleep. While he slept, he heard a voice telling him: 'Martin look in the street tomorrow. I will come to visit you.' Martin was excited. Could it be that Jesus was really coming to visit?

He looked intently on anyone who came near his shop. First came an old solider. He was poor and lived on charity. Today he had a shovel and began clearing away the snow. The work was too hard for him and he almost collapsed.

Martin brought him into his room and gave him a hot drink. Martin explained he was waiting for Jesus. But the old solider thanked him and told Martin he couldn't read and he knew nothing about Jesus.

After he left, Martin saw a young woman with flimsy clothes carrying a baby in her arms. She and the baby were shivering and close to collapse. Martin also brought her in from the cold. She was frightened by the old man with the spectacles on his nose. She explained she had no milk for the baby as she had not eaten herself. She had pawned her clothes earlier.

Martin gave her soup and bread and went upstairs and gave her the clothes in the wardrobe, which had never been used since his wife died. The woman was delighted and crossed herself and said, 'God Bless you.'

The day passed yet Martin did not meet Jesus. In the evening, an old woman came selling apples, she carried a bundle of sticks on her back. It was heavy, she was tired and it hurt. So she left it on the ground. As she did a young boy came racing past and quickly stole an apple.

She was furious and grabbed him before beating him. Martin went to the street and separated them. He told the old woman he would pay for the apple. He convinced the boy to ask for forgiveness and promise not to do it again.

He advised the old woman to forgive, because older people should be wiser and must lead by example. She thought about her own seven sons and the trouble they had got into and calmed down. She patted the boy on the head and let him go. She was about to pick up the sticks, but before she could the boy did it for her. 'Let me carry them granny,' he said. And off they went together, chatting as they went. And the old woman forgot to take the money for the apple.

Martin closed his shop that night frightfully disappointed that Jesus never came. Perhaps he only imagined he heard voices. By candlelight, he took his Bible down to read it. But before he did he nodded off to sleep.

As he awoke he heard footsteps. He turned around and there he saw a group behind him. 'It is I,' said the solider. 'It is I,' said the woman with the child. 'It is I,' said the woman and the young boy together.

Martin grew peaceful. He put on his spectacles and read the Bible at the open page in front of him.

'I was hungry and you gave me to eat, thirsty and you gave me to drink … As long as you did it to one of these my brethren you did it to me,' was what he read.

Martin now knew that Jesus did visit him. And what's more Martin had indeed welcomed him.

Core Practices for Thriving Parishes

2 December 2012

In her recent book, *Living into Community: Cultivating Practices That Sustain Us*, which carried out a comprehensive study into what helps a modern parish to continue to grow and flourish, Professor Christine D. Pohl concluded that thriving parishes share four core practices.

1. Communities should be encouraged to express deep *gratitude* for the many gifts they share. 'Grateful congregations are all too aware of the goodness, beauty and grace around them.' and readily, 'find opportunities to express gratitude and celebrate the gifts we have received.'

2. Good parishes are built on *trust*. Keeping promises is important. Healthy communities realise the pain of betrayal and understand the hurt that everyone experiences when organisations do not live up to their promises. Loyal communities Pohl writes, 'respond to church failures with patience, confession, correction, forgiveness and accountability'.

3. In good parishes people and families are encouraged to live with *integrity* and *truth*. Effective communities operate as transparently as possible. Doing so will lead to tensions and indeed the reality is that there will always be people to take advantage of the community's

vulnerability. However Pohl concludes that churches and communities grow when the hard issues are taken on honestly and directly and faced with clarity and focus.

4. Healthy communities are *welcoming* communities. 'The practice of hospitality is important not only for strangers and other vulnerable persons; it is also crucial for the life of the congregation itself. Hospitality is a means of grace for hosts as well as guests. Many people, after practicing hospitality comment that they 'got so much more than they gave' in welcoming a refugee family or in caring for a sick neighbour.'

'Often the best gift we can give another person is our time and attention. People come to life when they and their offerings are valued. This means that communities and the people in them must be willing to receive. Only as we recognise our own vulnerabilities and incompleteness are we open to what others can contribute,' Professor Pohl concludes.

What is heartening is that all four characteristics of a good parish are realistic and attainable. In fact they are common sense. As we all know grace builds on nature.

Queen Elizabeth in Enniskillen

1 July 2012

In November 1987, a treacherous bomb exploded in my home town, Enniskillen, killing eleven innocent people and maiming countless others, physically and emotionally.

The cowards who planted the bomb chose a group of God-fearing people remembering their war dead on a Sunday morning. For a few hours amidst the devastation, it seemed as if the quiet, peaceful county of Fermanagh would be forever divided in wasteful fighting. But due to the magnificent Christian message of Gordon Wilson and his family, good sense prevailed.

This was quickly followed by positive leadership from the local churches which kick-started the hard work of bringing the communities together. Gradually, the initiative led first to openness and then to a fragile unity.

Aware that once trust is broken it cannot be repaired, the communities gave birth to entirely new relationships between Catholics and Protestants.

There have been cross-community initiatives and inter-denominational services; there are projects to bring children out of their ghettoed past and into integrated education in the widest sense.

Today there is more tolerance and understanding than we could ever have imagined; it is wonderful to behold and a credit to community solidarity.

When everyone has something valuable to contribute, we all share something invaluable.

What we gained was there for all to see last Tuesday when Queen Elizabeth came to Enniskillen to partake in a service celebrating her Diamond Jubilee and to open one of the most modern and best-equipped hospitals in Europe.

She was welcomed, not by two communities working together, but by one united community who were proud of their town and county. There was no politicking. Catholics and Protestants celebrated in their churches and at their hospital without begrudgery.

Just how far we've come was clearly shown when Her Majesty joined clergy from all denominations in the Church of Ireland cathedral and then walked across the street with them to the Catholic Church. Everyone happily joined in; it was all done with great dignity and no fuss.

It could never have happened a few years ago. Now it has happened and every sensible person knows that's the way things should be and are going to be. It was all made possible when Elizabeth and Mary showed us how in Dublin. Like their namesakes in the gospel, Queen Elizabeth and President Mary concluded that nothing is impossible now. What a fantastic day for Enniskillen and Fermanagh. I'm glad I lived to see it.

THE NEED TO BE A PROPHET

In common usage the word 'prophet' is taken to mean somebody who can foresee the future. That is at best a half-truth. In scripture a prophet is someone who is different. A prophet can look at the present, interpret the signs of the times, and see in them hope for the present and a vision for the future. A prophet has to be fully immersed in the present times, understand them, listen to what the signs predict and hear the voice of God challenging us to a different, better future.

A prophet is someone who challenges the status quo and makes difficulties for the institution, someone who shakes things up and brings life to suffocating institutions.

In this view the prophet is almost always seen as an agitator. Some people like the prophet because he agitates. And some dismiss him as a troublemaker.

Probably a better way of putting it is, every prophet disturbs, but not everyone who disturbs is a prophet.

Fr Ronald Rolheiser, the philosopher and writer, suggests that, 'the effective prophet today is one who has a solid enough loyalty, a deep enough heart and extensive enough sympathy to hold together a community that is dangerously fragmented.'

There is, Rolheiser writes, too much division today. Good people are divided from good people. Committed people are divided from other committed people. There is anger, hatred, bitterness, blaming others, frustration and highly-selective loyalties. It's happening in society, in families and in churches.

A community divided against itself, where there are winners and losers, can never have God at its centre and will inevitably perish.

The simple virtues are easily forgotten. There has to be charity and respect for others. Good manners are necessary no matter how fractured communities are.

No cause, no matter how elitist, allows us to be uncharitable, disrespectful or bad mannered.

This too is the age of one issue journalists, one issue governments, one issue church people. This leads to false indignation, alienation among people and dissension in communities.

The genuine prophet is duty-bound to point out that some visions are destructive. A prophet allows the petty indignations to spend themselves like storms, to be followed by calm.

The liberals, the conservatives, the feminists, the bishops, the pro-life, the pro-choice, the survivor, the abuser, the puritan, the liberated, the legalist, the charitable, the socially concerned and the capitalist can sit down at one table. It is to take the scripture at its word 'In my Father's house there are many rooms.'

For that reason a prophet's vocation will inevitably be lonely and painful, distinguished by utter powerlessness. Rolheiser wrote, 'To be this kind of prophet is to sweat blood in the garden and to be powerless, defenceless and silent before those sat in the seats of both the left and the right.'

A prophet is dismissed by both sides. Judged to be too liberal by some, too conservative by others and too smug by most. A prophet will be called wishy-washy, a lightweight, a publicity seeker, lacking in commitment, unorthodox, judgemental and that awful phrase, 'One who lets the side down.'

With it comes the kind of loneliness which forced the Great Prophet to cry out from the cross, 'My God, My God why have You forsaken Me.'

The prophet will suffer because he'll inevitably be buffeted in the whirlwind of violence in society and in the church.

Who'd want to be a prophet?

DOROTHY DAY

13 November 2011

An outsider walking into some Christian churches could be forgiven for thinking that religion is an all-male affair. Many of the prayers are about God the Father and God the Son; quite frequently, the person who represents Christ at the altar – the priest – is a man.

Yet some of the most influential names in religion have been women. Women such as Mother Teresa of Calcutta, Mary Sumner, founder of the Mother's Union, and the fourteenth–century English mystic, Mother Julian of Norwich.

Anyone involved in the day-to-day running of a church knows that inevitably its women who are the backbone of every worthwhile activity in the community.

As Mary Kenny wrote, 'Religion may be patriarchal in its power structures. But it is women who spread it, women who keep it going, and women who are consoled by it.'

Without doubt the people who passed on the most meaningful spirituality to me were and are women. The vast majority of the leaders of our community here in Enniskillen where I work, are hugely dedicated women.

Before Mary McAleese became President, she frequently pointed out that the church needs to change with the times because, 'God has given us a rich garden to plant and grow; he's not given us a museum to preserve.' She often highlighted the value of prayer in the busy world of politics.

Of course, women in the Bible, play a major role in our salvation, from the time of Eve to the era of Mary the Mother of Jesus. Sarah for example, is an influential woman in the major faiths of Judaism, Christianity and Islam. Sarah is Abraham's wife, and in the New Testament both of them become symbols of faith, especially when life is difficult.

Today we still struggle to find ways whereby women's giftedness, freedom and responsibility can be nurtured and respected within the Christian churches – especially the Catholic Church. But I believe that every Christian community must nurture the God-given gifts of every member. If we don't carry out that basic challenge, we are failures.

One of the people who has inspired me greatly over the years is the American activist Dorothy Day. When Dorothy Day died in 1980 at the age of eighty-three, it was said that she was, 'The most influential, interesting, and significant figure in the history of American Catholicism.' Yet Day never held any office in the church and for most of her life, her ideas were almost universally rejected.

It was when she met a philosopher and agitator Peter Maurin, who encouraged her to spend her life helping the poor, that Day's life found its course. Maurin was a true prophet who believed it was not enough to denounce injustice. Dorothy Day believed that any act of love contributes to the balance of love in the world. And that any suffering endured in love, will ease the burden of others. I particularly like Day's assertion that, 'Our salvation depends on the poor. Yet food for the body is not enough. There must be food for the soul too.'

For nearly fifty years Dorothy Day tried to show that the radical commandment to love our fellow human beings should be part of our daily living.

For me Dorothy Day represented a revolutionary type of holiness – a way of serving Christ, not only through prayer, but through solidarity with the poor in their struggle for justice. As a result, she was regarded by many as a communist and was shot at, jailed and investigated repeatedly by the Federal Bureau of Investigation (FBI).

With typical insight she said she was even more disturbed by those who called her a saint. 'When they call you a saint,' she wrote, 'it means that you are not to be taken seriously.' For Dorothy, faith is not won without suffering. She once reflected, 'For me Christ was not to be bought with thirty pieces of silver, but with my heart's blood.'

THE EUCHARISTIC CONGRESS

24 June 2012

I was thrilled that the Eucharistic Congress went off so well. When it was first announced I was worried that it might become a painful reminder of that triumphant, powerful, male, clerical, church of the recent past. On the contrary the time I spent at the RDS and on the final day in Croke Park showed that many lay people, young and old, had taken on the responsibility of publicly displaying their faith through the many ways they served the community of visitors.

With remarkably few exceptions (two irate 'ladies' actually), the people were friendly, open, proud of their faith and most of all insistent that I should not change the way I speak and write about church affairs. Some day I'll tell you how much that changed my outlook – today it's only right to concentrate on the Congress.

It was with some fear and trepidation that I went to the RDS. I was even more frightened arriving in Croke Park. I felt that I couldn't join the great body of concelebrants lest they would see me as an embarrassment to the clerical church. So I sat in the stand.

It was a good decision for me personally because I felt at home with the young and old. But what helped me most was the huge number of people who promised me they were praying for me, especially when they receive the Eucharist. That was the special blessing God gave to me on Sunday last.

But enough about that part of my life. The Eucharistic Congress brought many believing, good, people together in a friendly, open way. There were no massive displays of power, yet enough good people turned out from around the country to let us know that there is still a wealth of goodwill towards the Catholic Church and the priests who minister to them.

People have come to realise that they hold the future faith of their family and church in their own hands. That's a massive step forward.

Archbishop Martin of Dublin was correct when he said that it should lead to all people (by which I presume he includes priests as well), to learn more about their faith and to trust more in the power of the Eucharist to transform us. That's a healthy spirituality.

The message from Pope Benedict comes from the same hymnbook. 'In a changed world, increasingly fixated on material things, you must learn to recognise in you the mysterious presence of the risen Lord, which alone can give breadth and depth to our life.'

There was a spirit of hope which can only come from genuinely sincere pilgrims. For some of the events, I was on duty for the BBC and was therefore more conspicuous than I wanted to be. But for most of it, I was able to wander around unnoticed like the lonely pilgrim I am these days.

In my wanderings I met Daniel O'Donnell. Daniel was there, not for notice, but to be part of the fifty thousand people in Croke Park. He sat on the pitch and sang and prayed as quietly as Daniel O'Donnell is allowed to sit and pray anywhere.

Mickey Harte was there too and I am sure he was praying for strength for his family in these terrible days. Undoubtedly he knew that in different circumstances his lovely daughter Michaela and her husband John would have been in Croke Park because they too were, in a good way, proud of their faith. To be honest one of the main intentions I prayed for at Croke Park was the Harte and McAreavey families. They have been asked to suffer more than any decent people should. My other intention was for families struggling to make ends meet during these troubled times.

I also met Declan Nearney. A few people shouted, 'Give us a song, Declan.' But Declan was more interested in an heirloom he inherited from his father who, back in 1932, had literally run a few miles to catch a train to go to Dublin. He collapsed on the train. But he did get there and received a memorial badge from the 1932 Congress. Declan was proudly wearing it on his chest in memory of his late father as he too made the same pilgrimage eighty years later.

Faith is deep in Irish people. The Eucharistic Congress was not an opportunity for them to proclaim that they were still Catholics, but to convince themselves they still have a place in a church that has become far too divided.

The people who were at The Eucharistic Congress last week have struggled through the bad old days when the church was powerful and oppressive. They are still struggling through when many in leadership speak a language they do not understand.

It is to the faithful people we should turn for support and guidance. It was those people who renewed my faith this week.

I was brought up to love the Eucharist as the centre of my life. Making Christ present is still the most mysterious part of my daily life. The joy of the Mass is what has kept me a priest when it would have been easier to walk away.

Last Sunday I was thrilled that the prayers of the people are encouraging me to stay.

Mission Sunday

21 October 2012

The range of choices for a Christian missionary is increasing every day as we understand more clearly what it means. As it so happened I was in London for a meeting this week and used the Underground daily. The adverts on the Underground, especially on the escalators, are a study in themselves. All sorts of things we should know about and many that we shouldn't know about, are on display. But one caught my eye. It was of a plastic statue of Jesus lying flat across the top of the poster. Long hair, beard, gentle, even effeminate looking, and certainly not the kind of man you'd put in as full-back on your local team. That's mainly how we have come to think of Jesus.

But the ad challenged a little more. It said, 'Dump your plastic Jesus. The real one is more interesting. Come to our church to learn about how the real Jesus loves you.'

I began to think that perhaps had I been in London this Sunday I would have visited that church. At least it's living in the real world. The last line added, 'He'll change your life.' You could hardly have a better introduction to mission than that.

Christian evangelisation should allow the word of God to change, help and bring peace to people, as well as bring dignity to them within their own culture and their own ambience.

Mission work now includes the lay volunteers who give a few months or a few years of their lives to serve the less well off. It also means somebody at home, each of us trying to stand up for what is right and what is just and suffering the consequences. It could mean speaking out for those who have no voice. It could mean organising people who are being used and abused here in our area. It's all part of the Christian missionary zeal. The values that Christ taught are to be spread in society wherever Christians choose to live. It's all part of putting the real Jesus in the place of the plastic Jesus who is too easily manipulated and used.

Yesterday I was in Dublin where Mary McAleese was launching her new book. It was a strange, large gathering of people as you'd expect for the former president.

She made a point which struck me as real. For the first time across the world, and particularly in Ireland, church authorities are having to deal with an educated laity, many of whom are more educated than the priests and the bishops themselves. She pointed out that when Vatican II started fifty years ago there wasn't even free education in the Republic of Ireland. Since Vatican II things have changed. As a lay and interested Catholic Christian who is proud of her faith and her church she wondered where the problem is in the church. She concluded it is at the level of governance.

She talked about the arrogance of the clerical church. She studied to become an expert in canon law; she then got a degree in canon law; she then went to Rome to get a licentiate to teach canon law, which she did at the Gregorian University. One day she was queuing for coffee dressed in jeans when a group of young clerics heavily dressed in Roman collars and shiny suits, spoke to her.

One of them asked her, 'What religious order are you?' with a little disdain, as she wasn't wearing her religious habit. She told them she wasn't a religious. His next question was, 'Are you a consecrated virgin, then?' to which she replied, 'Martin will be very surprised if I am.' This seemed to upset him terribly that a mere lay woman – not knowing that she was the former president of Ireland – would dare to teach canon law. She pointed out that Canon 212 invites and puts a duty on lay people to tell their pastor what they think. Anything she writes will be written in love because the church has officially invited her opinion. She asked the question, 'Are we free to live in truth if we are forced to live in silence?' That is what mission Sunday is about.

COMPASSION

I find it interesting today as we think of missionary activity and it is the feast of St Paul of the Cross who founded the Passionists.

St Paul of the Cross was an unusual man. It was said recently of Mother Teresa that she spent forty years of her life not knowing whether God existed or not. Paul of the Cross spent almost fifty years in the same position. It was only in the last weeks of his life that he was sure he had given his life for a good cause. For him the Passion of Jesus was what helped the poor and the suffering. He learned that from his own family. His father married twice and the second wife had sixteen pregnancies. Ten of the children died. So he knew what suffering was in his own family. He gathered companions around to simply retell the story of the Passion of Jesus and thereby give strength to the poor, the suffering, the neglected and the failures of this world by reminding them that the biggest failure of all was Jesus. His Resurrection means nobody is a failure.

St Paul of the Cross said that there were three things that we should do as Passionists:

1. Recognise that suffering is part of life.
2. Recognise that the power of the Passion and Resurrection will see us through even when we see no way through.
3. The Passion should inspire us to have compassion for anyone and everyone in every circumstance. Compassion should be the outstanding feature of the Passionist way of life.

I am not sure if any of this makes sense to you. But I know everyone here has to make choices in life. And that some of those choices were not what you wished for. There is nobody who hasn't felt a failure at some time. There is nobody who doesn't suffer outwardly and inwardly. There is nobody who doesn't need compassion themselves and therefore can pass on compassion to others.

It was Kahlil Gibran who said, 'We can forget those who laugh with us, but we will never forget those who cried with us.'

TIPPERARY PEACE PRIZE

15 July 2012

Last week I was at a most pleasant function in Tipperary when Professor Mary McAleese and her husband Martin McAleese jointly received the Tipperary Peace Prize. It was an uplifting and inspiring event where invited guests enjoyed the hospitality of this professional organisation.

I was invited to participate in their annual event on numerous occasions before, but this was the first year I was free to attend. It was a joyful occasion full of good cheer, good music, good food and good thoughts.

As usual Mary and Martin McAleese both made inspiring speeches dealing with their own path to peace. Interestingly both of them agreed that even during their days of courtship, they longed to bring about a culture of peace to Northern Ireland.

Martin was brought up in East Belfast. His was a Catholic family in a predominately Protestant area. 'The ambient atmosphere was one of fear, intimidation and sectarianism much of it real, some of it imaginary, but nonetheless all highly corrosive and detrimental to self-confidence and esteem,' he said in his revealing and personal speech.

'The imperative was to fade into the background, cover the badge on the school uniform, not wear the school tie except in school so as not to draw attention – anything not to be noticed. This was the nature of everyday living and the legacy of that for me, is a natural instinct to avoid the front row in many situations and to seek the anonymity of the back row.

'I was twenty when my family were forced out of our home in East Belfast during the early part of the Troubles. From then on I decided to live my life as if it were only beginning and rarely reflected on what went before.'

However, in later life, he began to respect the culture of people he once feared.

'To put the challenge differently, could we together find a way to move from a past characterised by two traditions and two communities, to a future still characterised by two traditions, but only one community at peace? To achieve this it was necessary to recognise, accept and respect our differences and to regard that diversity to be a source to utilise for the common good.

'But the important lesson from this small piece of my story is that the strongest and most enduring relationships, underpinned by trust and generosity, can be those whom we are least expected to befriend. There is no such thing as an impossible friendship; with friendship, nothing is impossible. For it is out of generous friendships and relationships that to our surprise, come the solutions to seemingly intractable problems … Working for peace is not just the preserve of specialists, but it's something we all can and should be involved in.'

Professor Mary McAleese related a simple story of how when her family were young they often went for walks around Rostrevor. One Sunday afternoon before their son Justin started school the children played together whilst Mary and Martin discussed deeper things. Suddenly Justin came running back to his mother and breathlessly asked; 'Mammy, you know this thing about Catholics and Protestants? Which are we? I've forgotten.'

And Mary went on to highlight that children aren't born bigots, prejudice doesn't come with our DNA. Both are learned through schools, communities, churches and parents. The work for peace begins at home.

This was the background to her opening principle: 'Everything that makes people hate and hurt is man-made.'

As a Christian, the work of peace is based on the gospel principle; love one another, especially our enemies. 'People have to make peace with their enemies … they cannot make it by oppressing each other into conformity or bombing each other into agreement.'

'What matters is that I want to be a good neighbour to my neighbour whoever he or she is, that I do not insist on being a good neighbour only to those who agree with me … I have an obligation to use the breath in my body to end the hatred that poisons successive generations and spreads its toxic spores in words, deeds and attitudes that have devastating consequences because we let it.'

Mary is convinced that, 'The best educated and most confident generation ever to inhabit this island brought to peacemaking a fresh creativity and intelligence, a generosity and a relentlessness that refused to give up no matter how tight the knot was being pulled in the opposite direction. Each death, each injury screamed failure and persistent failure became the fuel not of resignation or capitulation but of a humbler more determined search for answers that would stick.'

THE MYSTICS AND THE PROPHETS

5 February 2012

Karl Rahner who, it is often argued, was the greatest theologian of the past century, repeatedly said that the Christians of tomorrow will either be mystics or they will be nothing at all. All the unhealthy certainties of the past will disappear, forcing believers to discover the life and the love of God in the midst of their confused journey. For him the great love and the great suffering, which are essential parts of the mystic's way of life, open us to the unknowable.

Coincidently it was pointed out to me recently that the word 'mystic' is not even mentioned in the *Catechism of the Catholic Church.*

Those two statements, tell us why we need healing in and from the church today. For the church as we know it, with its structures and hierarchy, the language of faith can become dogmatic and abstract; it speaks to the head and not the heart. Rahner's conviction about the mystic's search was that we have to slow down to find God; or, more precisely, be found by God, in all the places we never thought of looking. Faith for the mystic, is not so much about what we believe; faith is about how to believe.

How to believe in a changing world is what many of the articles in this collection are about.

A criticism often voiced is that the official pronouncements of our church today don't relate to the world we believers live in. Many in leadership seem not to realise that religious practice is in decline and that the church as we know it has to change or face a slow death. Vocations to priesthood and religious life are in freefall. Many of those priests who struggle on in ministry are overworked and elderly; too many are crippled by cold celibacy.

The church's edicts are unsuited to the lives of people who find faith in new ways and in new places. We need a new way of expressing belief to make our faith come alive.

For so long as we continue to live in denial we are not likely to accept the Holy Spirit's promise to enlighten us. We will be trapped in tradition, unfree and unthinking.

Genuine healing will begin when theologians have the freedom to reflect, analyse, explore and teach. We need to kick-start transformation by encouraging a theology which is based on the insights of the Second Vatican Council.

It was during the Council that the Holy Spirit spoke with certainty and creativity. The problems which entomb us now are a direct result of the suppression of the Spirit of Vatican II. The cancer of clericalism has to be excised and an essential part of the treatment will be to affirm and encourage the church as the people of God.

Pastoral theology is in dire need of reform. Healing will take root when we welcome the 'infallibility' of the praying people of God. That in turn will inevitably lead to a spiritual renewal. The mystics will become the prophets.

In the scriptures the prophet is a professional inside critic – a protected species. Today's church excommunicates its prophets.

We will never solve the problems of tomorrow by returning to the mistakes of the past. There is no alternative to the insights of the Second Vatican Council and there doesn't need to be because that's where the Spirit lives.

Instead, today's reactive leadership often resorts to the theology of the ostrich – content to have a facade of unity or a superficial respectability. We have replaced the morality of the gospel with the legalism of injunction.

We forget that people have matured, that they think for themselves. They will not be treated like disobedient children.

Respect is a healing word. Respect for ourselves, respect for others – especially other people, other opinions and other churches.

In Christ's plan the mission of those chosen to lead the church is to recognise, affirm, and enable the work of the Spirit to flourish in the community. That's what the Christian mystic must do – abandon human kingdoms, trusting God to lead us to a holy place.

WE ARE A CHURCH, NOT A CLUB

9 June 2013

Despite the best efforts of hellfire preachers, I've always had doubts about the existence of hell. However whilst studying for the priesthood, I learned that to be a Catholic, I must believe in the existence of hell.

What hell consists of, or the severity of its punishment, is left entirely to the imagination. Fires that never go out and tortures that cannot be endured, are the result of those overzealous imaginations.

Just before ordination, I tried to deal with as many of my doubts as possible. I went to a righteous theologian and asked him about the existence of hell. He answered: 'We are bound to believe that hell exists, but we are not required to believe there is anybody in it.' It was a simplistic answer but it allowed me to set aside my scruples.

That incident came back to me during the week when I read what Pope Francis preached at a recent morning Mass for Vatican employees – namely that Christ redeemed the whole of humankind.

Pope Francis often asks questions of himself whilst preaching and then answers them. One of his questions was: Are atheists saved?

'Even the atheists,' he assured himself.

He used the word 'everyone' or its equivalent about twenty times in his informal homily. The Lord has redeemed all of us, everyone, with the Blood of Christ. And everyone means everyone not just Catholics. Pope Francis wasn't implying that all religions are of equal value. But he was affirming the power of Christ to save all humankind. His power cannot be limited.

It's a delightful pastoral approach in stark contrast to what we have endured in recent times from the Vatican. What Pope Francis said is true; we cannot limit the power of Christ to save humanity, or just to suit our own image of God. That's why the change in the words of Consecration at Mass is so hard to accept for many priests. For years we have prayed, 'It will be shed for you and for all for the forgiveness of sins.' The new missal forces us to limit the power of Christ's salvation by saying, 'Which will be poured out for you and for many for the forgiveness of sins.' Now Pope Francis reassures us that Christ died for all.

This reflects more truly what was proclaimed at the Second Vatican Council, 'The Catholic Church rejects nothing that is true and holy in these (other) religions,' because, 'they often reflect a ray of Truth which enlightens all men.'

This is one more example of how Pope Francis is showing himself to be a pastor opening up the gift of Christ to everyone. He allows God to be God and he wants the church to be a sign of God's mercy to all rather than be an exclusive club which arrogantly tells those who disagree, 'If you don't like the rules of the club you should get out.'

Pope Francis fully realises that he's a head of a church and not a club. He's probably aware too that in clubs, the members have a vote! More importantly the Pope assures us that God gives the gift of hope to everyone and not just to a few privileged clerics.

DREAM ON ...

March 2012

I'm not one who remembers dreams. I'm told we all dream, each and every night. But I seldom remember a dream. Once every couple of years maybe. But I did remember this dream.

It was disturbing and starkly visible. Most of the night, it seems to me now, was spent wrestling with a huge building. There were a lot of people in this structure which resembled a massive edifice like the Ballymun Flats. I was most agitated throughout the night, trying to get people into various rooms in this particular building. The top of the building was not completed and I was most anxious to raise money to roof the building. There were no sides in the building either. People burst out of sides too.

All my plans were constantly frustrated by a hyperactive, faceless individual whom I didn't recognise. As hard as I laboured to complete this building, he seemed equally intent on destroying it. Every time I got somebody into one room, he was driving them out and putting them in other rooms. I woke up, with the perspiration lashing off me and in a very agitated state.

After falling back asleep a second time, I suddenly realised that there was now a huge network of television aerials at the top of the building. The entire roof was covered in metal tubes, like a forest of antlers. So I presumed the building must be complete.

The next major reel that flashes back to memory has me sitting at a desk with an old-style archive typewriter. I looked up and I saw at the top of the building a wonderful joyous galaxy of people. Everybody was hanging out of the television aerials, gloriously happy and waving. There were people crowded into every visible space. Every room and window was full. There were huge numbers all moving together in unison giving the impression of being happy in victory.

Instantly my faceless friend appeared and whatever he did, right in front of my eyes, in a few seconds the building collapsed in an excellently-executed folding movement without any mess, no injuries, no deaths, without any fright, without any untidiness. It simply folded like an accordion and it, with the people in it, disappeared off the face of the earth.

Next he took my typewriter and smashed it into little bits. I can actually recall him rolling it up in a ball and dumping it in a basket. He also did the same to the computer. I was absolutely distraught.

All that was left on my desk was a crucifix. It became extremely vivid in my dream. The corpus was small, intricate and very clean, shining, even. The faceless friend then angrily picked up the crucifix and smashed it into little bits. I tried to prevent him, but was unable to do so. I was frightfully disturbed inside. Eventually he simply kicked the broken bits of the crucifix into a corner.

Still dreaming, I got up from the desk at that point because the phone was ringing. I went to answer the phone only to wake and find myself actually at my desk in my bedroom answering a phone nobody rang – so real was the dream. I now presume the phone was ringing in my dream. It is the story of my life in many ways. The phone always rings. That's where I was left with my dream.

I have been thinking a lot about it since and I haven't quite worked out what it all means. Instead of being upset by it, I in fact was greatly consoled. All the structures I have worked for in my life: completing buildings, completing programmes, making people happy, spending my life trying to get people in a position where they want to be, all the work in communication, all the writing and the TV work and the radio work – all of it may or may not be useful but it will collapse like an accordion or a deck of cards without much trace or meaning.

And who was my faceless friend? I don't know. But I think it was probably God directing me in a different way. Telling me that structures aren't important. Telling me that he is in charge if I'll only listen. Telling me too that all the writing will end up in a little ball in a wastepaper basket. And most of all telling me that preaching the Passion isn't about looking at a dead figure on a wooden crucifix. It's about dealing with people, listening to them, walking with them. It's about letting God be God. It's about answering his call.

HOPE SPRINGS ETERNAL

29 September 2013

If anything, the shock waves created by the interview Pope Francis gave to the Jesuit magazines are growing in intensity as the days pass. Despite the protestations of the extreme right here in Ireland and across the world, it is now clear that Pope Francis is determined to have a different style and a more compassionate church than what went before. In the interview he insisted that those who drag the church back in time have got it utterly wrong and must be resisted.

Secondly he wants a church which *lives* the values of the gospel of Christ.

Thirdly he contends that the conservative cardinals who gathered at the conclave earlier this year, gave him a mandate to purge the church of careerist clerics, corrupt institutions and the cynical politics which worked furiously against the Holy Spirit in undoing the principles of the Second Vatican Council.

Most importantly of all he wishes to proclaim the primacy of the gospel with its core message that Jesus Christ died to save everyone and not just a select few.

I am almost afraid to allow myself believe there has been such a sea change within a few months.

As a matter of interest I rechecked the letter of censure which my Superior General received from the Congregation for the Doctrine of Faith in 2010. Five issues which they condemned me for, and warned that if I did not change my opinion on I would be silenced and eventually excommunicated, are now being proposed by Pope Francis himself. I have not felt so much at peace in over a decade.

Pope Francis began by admitting that he himself is a sinner in need of redemption, 'I am a sinner whom the Lord has looked upon,' he said.

On the other hand I have found it difficult to understand why it is that the Pope, in proclaiming the centrality of the gospel of Jesus Christ, should make world headlines for doing so. It proves that what has been wrong within the institutions of the church has overshadowed the gospel to such an extent that it is now a surprise when the Pope proclaims his belief in the message of the gospel.

'My style of government as a Jesuit at the beginning had many faults,' he admits. 'I made my decisions abruptly and by myself. My authoritarian and quick manner of making decisions led me to have serious problems and to be accused of being ultra-conservative.' But Pope Francis learned from his failures as all of us should. Learning from past mistakes is a necessary part of any spiritual journey. So is believing oneself to be a sinner embraced by God's love.

As Pope, discernment will be central to his governance. He believes what Blessed John XXIII said, 'See everything; turn a blind eye to much; correct a little.'

For the Pope discernment cannot be rushed: 'Many think that changes and reforms can take place in a short time. I believe that we always need time to lay the foundation for real effective change and this is the time for discernment. Discernment is always done in the presence of the Lord, looking at the signs, listening to the things that happen, and to the feelings of the people, especially the poor.'

There will be no rash judgements, no quick changes. It's a wise policy and shows the Pope is sincere.

Doubt is also part of the spiritual life: 'If a person says that he met God with total certainty and is not touched by a margin of uncertainty, then that is not good ... If one has answers to all the questions – that is the proof that God is not with him. It means that he is a false prophet using religion for himself.'

Pope Francis is not impressed by those Catholic writers – lay and clerical – who ruthlessly condemned those with a different point of view to them over the years and who now instantly changed their minds, pretending that they always held the views which Pope Francis now preaches.

The Pope's image of the church, 'Is that of a holy, faithful people of God. The church is the people of God on the journey through history with joys and sorrows.' He goes on to re-emphasise what was a particular theme of the Vatican Council, namely, 'All the faithful, considered as a whole, are infallible in matters of belief … this infallibility in believing, through a supernatural sense of the faith of all the people walking together … is genuine and is assisted by the Holy Spirit … we should not even think therefore that "thinking with the church" means only thinking with the hierarchy of the church.'

Again that in effect, will put an end to the evil of clericalism.

The Pope foresees an accusation which the ultra-right always make, namely that these views are populism at its worst: 'If the Christian is a restorationist, a legalist, if he wants everything clear and safe, then he will find nothing. Tradition and memory of the past must help us to have the courage to open up new areas to God. Those who today always look for disciplinarian solutions, those who long for an exaggerated doctrinal "security", those who stubbornly try to recover a past that no longer exists – have a static and inward-directed view of things.'

Pope Francis believes that if the church doesn't change it will collapse like a house of cards. Perhaps he held back from stating the obvious – that it has already collapsed in the sense that it has failed the very people whose faith kept it going.

The Pope is obviously a man who believes that we can all be 'surprised by the Spirit'.

Personally one of the most helpful insights the Pope communicated was the difference between optimism and hope. Optimism can be useful but can also help us to live in denial.

Hope admits the reality of darkness but trusts God to see us through.

Pope Francis has certainly begun a journey of hope for people of goodwill. The middle Catholics who despise the trickery of ultra-conservatives and don't trust the ultra-liberals, have at last found a voice.